T0023360

"When you find yourself underli[...]
whole book is basically one long u[...]
that book. Highly. And be gratefu[...]

> —**Lenore Skenazy**, president of Let Grow, and founder of
> Free-Range Kids

"Pathological social withdrawal (called 'hikikomori' in Japan) is now increasingly considered a global mental health and socioeconomic concern. Withdrawal behaviors tend to be regarded as negative and maladaptive. Is this perception always correct? Randy Paterson's book challenges such preconceptions and prejudices regarding hikikomori-related behaviors while also suggesting multidirectional solutions to this phenomenon."

> —**Takahiro A. Kato, MD, PhD**, associate professor
> in the department of neuropsychiatry, and chair of the
> hikikomori research clinic at Kyushu University Hospital
> in Fukuoka, Japan

"Innovative and inspiring.... The provocative mood makes the reading easy; the structure in lessons makes the book an on-demand pool of instructions the reader can refer to whenever needed. Randy Paterson has made great work to collect life situations and convert them into such practical actions."

> —**Ivan Ferrero, PsyD**, cyberpsychologist, speaker, trainer,
> educator, edge innovator, and futurologist

"Randy Paterson has done it again! In his latest book, *How to Be Miserable in Your Twenties*, Paterson provides insight into how young adults can avoid common traps that can contribute to unhappiness. It includes a range of well-tested, commonsense strategies that are especially relevant for those transitioning into adulthood and independence. This engaging and humorous book is a must-read for young adults (even those who are not in their twenties) who want to prevent the thoughts, behaviors, and habits that can lead to feeling overwhelmed, depressed, or anxious. I highly recommend it!"

—**Martin M. Antony, PhD, ABPP**, professor in the department of psychology at Ryerson University in Toronto, ON, Canada; and coauthor of *The Shyness and Social Anxiety Workbook* and *The Anti-Anxiety Workbook*

"*How to Be Miserable in Your Twenties* reads with a tender irreverence. Paterson's voice is heart-catching, imaginative, and wise as he invites emerging adults to abandon many of their self-defeating delusions which they have caught from their culture like a virus. Paterson gifts the reader with fresh agility to better dance with the paradoxical vicissitudes of life. You will find his creative re-rendering of the path to misery accessible, charming, and a helpful tool for reorienting you to a wise life."

—**Scott Spradlin, LPC, LMAC**, dialectical behavior therapy (DBT) therapist and trainer in Wichita, KS; and author of *Don't Let Your Emotions Run Your Life*

HOW TO BE MISERABLE

IN YOUR

TWENTIES

40 STRATEGIES TO FAIL AT ADULTING

RANDY J. PATERSON, PhD

NEW HARBINGER PUBLICATIONS, INC.

Publisher's Note

This publication is designed to provide accurate and authoritative information in regard to the subject matter covered. It is sold with the understanding that the publisher is not engaged in rendering psychological, financial, legal, or other professional services. If expert assistance or counseling is needed, the services of a competent professional should be sought.

Distributed in Canada by Raincoast Books

Copyright © 2020 by Randy J. Paterson
     New Harbinger Publications, Inc.
     5674 Shattuck Avenue
     Oakland, CA 94609
     www.newharbinger.com

Cover design by Amy Shoup
Acquired by Tesilya Hanauer
Edited by Teja Watson

All Rights Reserved

FSC
MIX
Paper
FSC® C011935

Library of Congress Cataloging-in-Publication Data on file

Printed in the United States of America

22 21 20

10 9 8 7 6 5 4 3 2 1   First Printing

For Geoff,
who wasn't there that decade.
Which is just as well.

Most of the harm done in the world is done by those who think they know what happiness is for other people and try to help them achieve it.

—Quentin Crisp

I believe that maturity is not an outgrowing, but a growing up: that an adult is not a dead child, but a child who survived.

—Ursula K. Le Guin

It's adult swim time and I'm diving in here at the shallow end.

—Suzanne Finnamore

Contents

The Great Leap Forward

Many who seem to be struggling with adversity are happy; many, amid great affluence, are utterly miserable.

—Tacitus

Why misery? Why the twenties?

Well. Get in the car.

Drive the narrow highway north of Vancouver. Pass the smooth black lake—the one no one ever seems to swim in, perhaps fearing what lurks beneath the surface. Glance ahead, where the road slashes between rock faces and disappears, the mountains on the far side of Howe Sound a distant barrier.

It's a crest and curve. The road sweeps to the right, rejoins the coastline, and one of the largest granite domes on Earth comes into view: the Chief. Seven hundred meters. Mostly straight up.

There's your climb.

No rush. You've got seventy years. Or eighty. A hundred if you're lucky.

Divide it up any way you like. Psychologist Erik Erikson described it in eight stages, from infancy to old age.[1]

There are challenges relevant to the whole effort. Are you dressed right? Pacing yourself? Properly equipped?

A while back I published *How to Be Miserable: 40 Strategies You Already Use*, a guidebook to the hazards along life's trajectory. There are many more than forty ways to sabotage our contentment, of course, so I made my choices for their wide applicability—their effectiveness at producing disaster at any age.

There are also challenges specific to each stage, however. That rock over there to your left? Don't stand there: it's loose. That steel ring? Ignore it—my buddy put it in; he's an idiot. That shelf? Solid; you can trust it.

Perhaps no phase offers more traps than the crumbling overhang known as the twenties—especially now, as our century negotiates its own dysfunctional early adulthood. Faltering economies, crumbling certainties, light-speed technological change, ever-morphing professions. Many of the holds here don't hold, the guidebooks are upsidedown, the cracks are chasms, and the arrows were drawn by jokers, optimists, inspirational speakers, and pharmaceutical representatives sniffing for profit. You're supposed to…

- Choose between remaining with family or striking out (and maybe, yes, *actually* striking out) on your own.

- Find a career path on a shifting economic iceberg that submerges entire fields every few years.

- Figure out which of those shiny, self-affirming slogans about adult life are valid and which are happy-sounding codswallop.

- Renovate your own personality to fit independent life, despite having spent most of your upbringing in human obedience training.

- Know, as the song says, when to hold 'em and when to fold 'em, walking the tightrope between sensible caution and necessary risk.

What are the odds of nailing all this and more? Just about nil. Time, then, for a consideration of the landmines awaiting us at the dawn of our newfound maturity.

But first, a touch of background.

IN THE BEGINNING

In my first few years after graduation I avoided filling my practice with people suffering from depression. I'd veered uncomfortably close to it myself during my training years. Then fate, with its usual backhanded sense of humor, handed me the leadership of a depression treatment program for people who had recently been discharged from inpatient care.

We ran groups in the cheerless basement of the hospital. The idea was to train people in the basics of cognitive behavior therapy (CBT) and coach them to apply the principles in their own lives. Realizing that most of the clients had already been through multiple failed treatments, I chose not to waltz in with pom-poms flailing, shouting cheers of praise about the wonders of exercise and social contact. They would have shot me down in an instant.

Instead, I took them in a direction they were not expecting. I asked what they would do if their mission was to feel even worse, not better. I offered the incentive of an imaginary $10 million if they could manage it for even a morning.

After some hesitation, they started offering ideas: stay in bed, close the curtains, call in sick to work, play hurtin' songs, watch daytime television, binge on junk food. They got competitive, talking over one another. "Sit naked in front of a full-length mirror!" "Call my mother!" "Reconnect with my ex!"

Then I asked how many of these things they were already doing, or were tempted to do when they awoke with depression as a companion. *Stay in bed. Close the curtains. Call in sick. Scoop into the mocha chip for breakfast.*

Perhaps their low mood wasn't such a mystery. They were already living many elements of the life they'd adopt if they wanted the misery money. This was bewildering, because the prize was imaginary and they truly, truly, truly did not want to be depressed. Their curiosity was sparked.

The striking feature of this gambit was that it was so easy. If I asked people mired in misery how they might feel better, most were stuck for ideas. When I asked them how to feel worse, the strategies flew off the tongue.

Big deal, you're thinking. *Who wants to feel worse?*

I have a place in the dry ranchland of British Columbia, and I often take guests up a sagebrush-strewn embankment to a lookout. I always have problems finding the animal track that leads up the slope. Eventually I stumble across it and look back down: there's the beaten-down grass of the trail, obvious for anyone to see. The way up and the way down are the same path, but the way down is easier to find.

The same is true of mood and life. Whole industries (entertainment, travel, cannabis, psychopharmacology, self-help publishing) are devoted to finding the elusive passage to happiness. But if you find the road to misery, you've found the road to fulfillment as well. Just turn right rather than left. If isolating makes us worse, then maintaining a reasonable social life helps us out. If avoiding things that scare us makes us more fearful, then facing them builds our courage.

We spend each day making decision after decision. What will I have for breakfast? Which route to the office? Which project will I work on first? Where do I want to live? Buy or rent? Where do I want to go on holiday? Who should I marry? Sourdough or rye?

All of these decisions have a common feature: at some level, they are about how to feel better in the future. If I get my taxes done tonight, then tomorrow I can relax and enjoy life a bit more. If I study for the math final, I'll be more likely to get a decent grade and won't have to retake the course, which will be a happy relief. If I pee now, the road trip will be infinitely more comfy.

We spend most of our lives trying to make things better. We look at existence from that one perspective and, yes, it works to some extent, but we still step in the poop, we're not nearly as happy as our external circumstances would seem to warrant, and when we look back we can spot some obvious missteps that we should have foreseen.

Spend ten thousand hours staring at a problem, and what are the odds that another hour will turn up the solution? Look at it from a new angle, however—even one that seems wrong—and insights may cha-cha out from the shadows. If you get stumped putting together an Ikea dresser, turn it over and look underneath. That's probably where the missing bolts have been hiding. So—what if misery was your goal, instead of joy?

I used my experience with the therapy group as the core of a talk I gave to the local library, billing it as "How to Be Unhappy."

I reasoned that no one would show up and I could go home early. The touchingly optimistic event host had laid out two hundred chairs. Five minutes before I was due to begin she was frantically putting out more, and still there were people standing at the back. I offered the talk again. And again. A publisher surfing ads for psychology-related topics saw the announcement and suggested a book. And here we all are.

A SHADE OF GREY

Most writers are narcissists.

Amazon, ever the enabler of bad habits, feeds and nurtures this toxic tendency. You've probably noticed the "Bestsellers Rank" beneath each book, indicating its current sales position. (There are two types of author in the world: those who say they look at this figure, and those who lie.) There is also a behind-the-curtain site that lets you track your sales from week to week.

One day I was indulging this secret vice and saw that sales of *How to Be Miserable* had shot upward unexpectedly. I did some Internet searching and discovered the explanation: a month or two earlier I had received an email requesting permission to post a short YouTube video about a few of the concepts in the book. I had granted this, asking only that the developer at least mention the name of the book from whence they came. Then I forgot all about it.

If I were more plugged in to popular culture I would have recognized the name on the email: C.G.P. Grey, one of YouTube's most-followed vloggers. His video had gone live, and within a day or two it had racked up more than a million views, which swelled to more than three million in the following weeks.[2]

Grey had chosen some of the most basic ideas in the book: get no exercise, eat garbage food, randomize your sleep schedule, set vague and unrealistic goals, stay at home, and a few more. He had set them to music and illustrated the result with his signature stick figures.

I liked the video, but I was more fascinated by the thousands of comments cascading beneath. A few had posted remarks like "I do all this stuff and am perfectly happy" or "Why would anyone do this?" Far more, though, expressed rueful recognition:

- "Stop describing my life."

- "Looks like I'm on the right track."

- "I unintentionally do almost all of these steps every day. Funny, right? Right?"

- "Have you been spying on me?"

- "Holy crap, I do 90 percent of this without realizing it. It's as if he was reading my mind."

Huge numbers of Grey's viewers seemed to spend their lives sitting at home watching YouTube videos, feeling stuck and dissatisfied.

No surprise there. YouTube viewers are mostly avid Internet consumers, and logically, those who are at home watching tend to be those who stay home and watch. It's not unlike conducting a survey at a gym and discovering that most of your respondents work out, or at a bar and finding heavy drinkers, or at a hotel and finding mostly travelers. Still, the frequency with which people saw a mirror instead of a video was unsettling.

This echoed my experience in the clinic. Ever since starting my practice I've seen people who describe their days of isolation, inactivity, and lack of structure or purpose, and their corresponding emotional lives of boredom, lethargy, and emptiness.

One man gave me the full rundown on his daily life: Wake up in early afternoon, flick on the TV, scrounge for food, smoke up, surf the Net, heat something in the microwave, update Instagram, watch a movie, see no one face-to-face, head to bed. No reason to get up or go anywhere; no partner, few friends, no job, only sporadic activities. His mood was low. He thought he had a brain disorder.

Slightly overcaffeinated at the time, I impulsively blurted out, "But that's how a life like that feels." It was conceivable that he might have a neurological problem (he didn't), but this wasn't necessary to explain his mood. I mimicked striking my thumb firmly with a hammer. "If you do that and feel pain, your thumb isn't doing anything unusual. It's responding completely normally. When people live this way, that's the emotion that comes with it."

It was tempting for my client—and, I'm sure, for many of Grey's YouTube viewers—to attribute the life he was living to the emotions he felt. With a mood that low, how could he do anything else? What he wasn't seeing was that the life he had adopted was also perpetuating his low mood and lack of motivation and interest. His emotions, behavior, and ways of thinking were locked in a downward spiral.

So, if we're trying to change things, where do we start? Answer: wherever we can. There aren't many interventions that get rid of sadness, emptiness, or lethargy right at the outset. So we work on the life instead. Get a bit more exercise, for example, and energy levels tend to rise. Sleep improves, producing better daytime concentration, which enables a sharper focus on getting things done, which reduces the feeling of being a burden while building confidence, which makes social interaction more likely, ultimately making it easier to ramp up the exercise a bit more. We create a positive spiral, with small changes reverberating around the life and producing knock-on effects. We give up on solving the mood problem, and work on the life problem instead.

The dividing line between most mood problems and the rest of human existence is largely artificial. Although some people do experience genuine brain disorders, most of the distress seen in psychological clinics is understandable once we assess the life the person has been living and the way they think about it. What's true for most diagnosable mood states tends also to be true for garden-variety unhappiness or misery.

WHAT'S THIS GOT TO DO WITH THE TWENTIES?

In *How to Be Miserable*, I reverse-engineered the treatment literature for depression to come up with useful ideas for the rest of us. But I was focused on total life span concepts: strategies that lower the mood regardless of one's age. As I mentioned in the opening to this discussion, there are also considerations specific to each of life's stages, and nowhere is this more true than in the early years of adulthood.

Part of the problem is that from birth we are raised to be children. That's why they call it child-rearing. And what's the mission of a child? Understanding the rules and following the lead of a nearby adult. Then, around the age of thirteen, someone abruptly says to us, "Don't be so childish." Well, why not? That's what we were raised to be. Don't sculpt a teapot in pottery class and then cast it aside because, oh look, it's a teapot. That's what you wanted!

They train us to be children, then change their minds and want us to be adults instead. You're supposed to negotiate this switchback on life's highway while your body, long reliable but a little taller every year, becomes alien even to you. Your brain sits in a hormonal soup that starts out as Mrs. Boring's Chicken Noodle and suddenly becomes Thai Tom Yum Goong—with fire peppers, Viagra, and hallucinogenic mushrooms.

Then, you come out of that tunnel into your twenties, filled with reams of contradictory advice. People take turns alternately wanting to stuff you back into childhood or refusing to give any advice at all—because, hey, you're an adult and should know this stuff already.

There's a strange thing about life stages. They proliferate like bunnies. You start with two—childhood and adulthood—and before you know it they've subdivided. Adolescence (from the Latin *adolescere*, to grow up) wasn't originally considered a separate stage. It was a punctuation mark between childhood and adulthood. Then G. Stanley Hall, an early American psychologist, fleshed it out in his 1904 opus called, unsurprisingly, *Adolescence*.[3] He characterized it as a stage of its own, distinguished by wonky mood, attention-seeking, risky behavior, and conflicts with parents.

A new stage, of course, means a new transition—this time between adolescence and adulthood—and a century after Hall's book the term *adultescence* has come into vogue. This vaguely pejorative word can be applied to a person of any age pretending to be part of youth culture—think the pigtailed elderly at summer music festivals—or a person years past puberty who hasn't quite become independent. It suggests immaturity in the person being discussed, balanced by a wee bit of envy in the observer. As a period of study, though, adultescence is tied more closely to age—usually from nineteen to twenty-nine.

A useful term for researchers, maybe. But is it necessary? It's a syllable longer than "young adult," so we can't claim it's a short form. *Adultescent* (and the equally obnoxious *kidult*) is a not-so-subtle way of hiding an insult behind a mock-clinical term, and a way of excluding someone from the not-so-coveted club of adults by implying that they haven't quite passed the entry exam.

Nevertheless, there's something distinct about this, as about all life stages—and much of the distinction lies in the sheer number of ways that things can go sideways.

MINEFIELD OR PARADISE?

There are two ways of thinking about young adulthood, and they're both wrong.

The first is that it should be impossible to be miserable during this time.

- Your life expectancy is just about as high as any society on Earth has ever been able to manage. You have decades of mileage left on the ticker.

- The odds are pretty good that you have your health.

- You probably haven't had time to put yourself in really insurmountable debt (though student loans are an excellent start).

- You haven't yet snookered yourself with multiple conflicting responsibilities.

- Smallpox, polio, mumps, and typhoid are all but over, and even HIV is reasonably controllable.

- If you live in a developed economy, the risk of starvation is low, food is plentiful, and beds are comfortable and relatively bug-free.

- Millions of people spend their lives creating online content, the only function of which is to entertain you.

- The availability of contraception means you are probably not going to be forced into celibacy or accidental parenthood.

Even by the standards of royalty of past ages, most of us are not simply privileged—we live in actual paradise. We have microwave ovens, streetlights, vision correction, and buffalo wings. We should be flatly incapable of misery. Yet we aren't.

The alternative point of view is that misery should be inevitable.

- Weapons exist that could obliterate you and everyone you love at any time.

- Humans have managed to so pollute the Earth that its capacity to sustain life is in question.

- We have proliferated to the extent that we are crowding out most other species—including many upon whose survival we depend.

- The gluttony and carelessness of past generations is yours to correct or suffer from.

- The planet-bound frontiers humans have dreamed about for millennia have mostly been explored, and the extraterrestrial ones are almost certainly beyond your means.

- Our leadership is often slow, inadequate, and self-serving, or panders indecently to the worst instincts of the mob.

- Technology, now seductive to the point of addiction, means that millions spend most of their days staring at screens.

- Wages in many countries have been stagnant since U2 last had a decent album.

From this perspective, misery should be impossible to escape.

Yet it isn't. The overwhelming majority of young adults do not suffer from clinical depression, despite a trend toward the overdiagnosis and overmedication of normal-range emotional turmoil. People continue to build their skills, build their friendship networks, build their relationships, and live their lives.

The truth is more complicated, as is so often (and so inconveniently) the case. There are many factors that make life easier and pleasure more accessible than in previous generations. There are others that impose or intensify new challenges. Both misery and happiness remain available to most, and almost all will experience a blend of the two.

HOUSTON, ARE YOU SURE WE HAVE A PROBLEM?

Epidemiological data throughout the developed world show an upswing in mental health concerns among people in their twenties and late teens. The average age of first onset of depression, for example, was formerly thought to be around age thirty. More recently, it seems to appear most often in the early twenties. Further, these early-adulthood depressions don't seem to be fleeting periods of gloom. Severe depression seems to be more common than it once was, and recurrences are more frequent.

Anxiety disorders, by contrast, do not appear to be changing in their prevalence—but this observation masks a troubling reality. Anxiety disorders, taken as a group, make up the largest category of mental health problems in the population, and they are most common in younger adults.[4]

About one-third of the population is likely to meet diagnostic criteria for an anxiety disorder in their lifetime, and prevalence appears to be highest in the twenties, with declines thereafter. Most such disorders have their median age of onset early in life: social anxiety disorder at thirteen, agoraphobia without panic attacks at twenty, and panic disorder at twenty-four.

Oh, and let's not even talk about the addictions, most of which really get their groove on in the twenties.

Diagnosable mental disorders represent only part of the picture, however. Many clinicians (of which I am one) are unimpressed by the efforts of the mental health "industry" to brand problems as illnesses, as if there were a blood test to distinguish them from normal-range functioning. In the case of mumps, for example, you either have it or you don't. Vanishingly few of the "disorders" listed in the *Diagnostic and Statistical Manual* (DSM, now in its fifth edition, hence DSM-5[5]) represent such clear and qualitatively distinct entities.

Instead, most disorders are simply more severe or troubling versions of normal human experiences. We all have periods of sadness, sleep disruption, lack of energy, and poor concentration, all of which can be symptoms of major depressive disorder—or of twenty-first-century life. We all concern ourselves with what others may think of us, as in social anxiety disorder. We all feel compelled to cuddle up in the safety of home, as in agoraphobia. We worry about things that may never happen, as in generalized anxiety disorder. The people charged with creating the DSM sit around a boardroom table, draw a line in the continuum of distress, and call one side of the line normality and the other disorder.

Normal (bell-shaped) frequency curves bulge in the middle and taper at the extremes. If we define disorder as being out at the skinny end, then across the imaginary border in normal-land the curve gets much fatter: there are far more people living there. So there are always many more cases in the "troubled but not quite enough to call it a disorder" range. If one-third will meet criteria for an anxiety disorder at some point in their lifetime, and one-tenth to one-fifth for a depressive disorder, then far more than that will experience emotional challenges strong enough to derail them—and these derailments occur disproportionately in the twenties.

A NEET LITTLE ISSUE

Sit like a fly on the wall of my consulting room and watch what happens.

Over and over again, I assess a young adult and find they are living at home with one or both parents, stuck in the crack between adolescence and adulthood, under- or unemployed, fearful of rejection or failure, with a narrow or nonexistent social life, not dating, not traveling, not exploring, not progressing in their own goals and often uncertain what those goals might be. It is as though they have aged out of adolescence but haven't been able to negotiate the transition to the next phase of life.

Some years ago, I began asking the groups of mental health professionals attending my training programs whether they were seeing a lot of clients like this. Routinely, more than half raise their hands. So I began to focus my practice on this group, and searched the medical literature for treatment studies that might guide my efforts. No dice.

I was looking in the wrong place. I should have been consulting the sociological and cross-cultural literature. In country after country, a similar phenomenon has been identified. Most of the studies are descriptive in nature. They focus on the numbers and characteristics of people falling into the ill-defined category—but not on how to help them move on.

Virtually everywhere, local authors give the phenomenon a local name—and in the vast majority of cases they fail to link it with the similar population a country or a language away. The names are often insulting. In Italy they are *bamboccioni*—"big babies." In Spain they are *Generation Ni Ni*, alluding to "no education, no employment." In the United Kingdom they are either *NEETs* (Not in Education, Employment, or Training) or *KIPPERS* (Kids in Parents' Pockets Eroding Retirement Savings). In the US the term is "failure to launch," with that enormous word, *failure,* right up front.

Nowhere in the world is the phenomenon discussed as much as in Japan, where they are *hikikomori* (literally, "pulling inward" or "being confined"). Estimates vary, but a 2016 survey by the Japanese government suggested that there were more than 540,000 people in such a situation in the country of 126 million.[6]

Although this represents less than 0.5 percent of the Japanese population, the phenomenon is disproportionately prevalent in the young-adult age group, representing a much higher proportion of twentysomethings. Further, these figures say nothing about the number of young people experiencing other problems (including anxiety disorders and depression) but not shutting themselves away from the world.

Whether in Japan, Spain, or the United States, these are not young people making the reasonably sensible decision to remain in the family home and enjoy life rather than overspending on rent. They seem trapped, unhappy, stuck—while the clock of their lives continues to tick.

The cross-cultural literature is fascinating for its biases. Researchers from North America jet into other societies and immediately attribute the problems they find to the pathologies of the cultures they are examining. This is glaringly evident in the non-Japanese literature about Japan, where the dominant question seems to be "What is so weird about Japanese culture that it produces these stay-at-homeboys?" Well, nothing. Take a look in your own basement.

The hikikomori problem includes an epidemiological puzzle. In virtually every survey, every study, every informal sampling of clinicians, the majority of people who fit within this fuzzy category are men. The Japanese government study suggested that about two-thirds were male. My experiences in Canada would suggest something more like 80 percent male to 20 percent female, an estimate echoed by the clinicians I have asked.

Why males? "Wage stagnation," suggested one workshop attendee. Well, yes, the income of young men has been quite flat in recent decades, whereas that of young women has been rising. This hasn't put women ahead, however; it has only narrowed the gender gap. Young men still make more than young women on average. It should be easier for males to strike out into the world, but it is more often their sisters who are casting off and sailing away from home port.

So why else? One possibility—sexist but probably true—is that young women are taught more self-care skills like cooking, laundry, and budgeting than men are, so they're more equipped to leave home. Another may be that more women look to the instrumental nature of early jobs (will this pay the rent?), whereas young men are exhorted to pursue hard-to-find passions or establish their status with their employment. Still another may be the shifting and contradictory expectations placed on twenty-first-century males. Whatever the reason, kick-starting adulthood seems to be increasingly difficult—and the evidence suggests that more males are having ignition issues.

It's tempting to think that I am just pathologizing the decision to stay home with the 'rents. Not so. In many cultures, remaining at home when young is entirely expected. European statistics indicate that 66 percent of Italian young adults aged eighteen to thirty-four live with at least one parent (73 percent of males, 60 percent of females).[7]

The figures are lower in the US (40 percent of males, 38 percent of females in 2016[8]) and UK (42 percent of males, 31 percent of females), while the phenomenon is less common in Scandinavian countries such as Denmark (22 percent of males and 17 percent of females).

Since when was a multigenerational household a mental health crisis? Staying at home isn't the problem. It's being stuck at home, spinning their wheels and getting nowhere. It's C. G. P. Grey's audience saying, "I live like this, and I hate it."

THE PARENTHESES OF CIRCUMSTANCE

When I first wrote *How to Be Miserable*, I was concerned that some readers would see it as blaming the victim. Here's what to do if you want to feel worse—and look: you're already doing it, so bam, it's your own fault. But the few people who have raised this objection seem to have been reacting to media coverage, not the book itself. When people read between the covers they see that there is no blame given.

In that book, I made a distinction important enough to repeat here. Misery is brought about by two types of influence: Column A and Column B.

Column A consists of the many factors influencing our mood over which we have no control. Asteroid strikes, tsunamis, economic collapses, the deaths of loved ones, friends moving away, employers going bankrupt, cars getting rear-ended, DNA manifesting diseases, getting born into dysfunctional families, and so on. Add to these all the unwelcome events that you might have prevented had you not missed the chance: exams you failed, relationships that imploded, accidents you caused, addictions you fed. You don't own a time machine, and can't go back and choose another universe.

Here are a few societal Column A factors that apply to many in their twenties:

- In lots of cities (including San Francisco, Seattle, New York, Vancouver, Toronto, Sydney, London, Paris, and others) rents are sufficiently high that independent living is profoundly difficult for those in entry-level jobs without multiple roommates and bunk beds.

- Post-secondary education in many countries, especially the US, has become increasingly unaffordable, potentially shutting out people from less-privileged backgrounds and leaving graduates with heavy debt loads.

- The divide between rich and poor has been widening in most developed economies—again, most markedly so in the US—resulting in a small overclass of privilege with a much larger underclass for whom wages and buying power has largely stagnated since the 1970s.

- The job market is increasingly made up of short-term contracts, meaning that the security (but also stultification) of lifetime job tenure is harder to come by; workers are consequently faced with making job decisions constantly, rather than just at the outset of a career.

- Prognostications about environmental and climate degradation have left many with a pessimistic outlook about their own future—and a disinclination to produce children who may experience worse to come.

- The Internet has disrupted many forms of social interaction, making traditional friendships and support more difficult for many to find—and making anonymous online bullying and harassment a regular occurrence.

- Even some seemingly positive developments, like the increasing diversity of options in career, mobility, and lifestyle, can impose decision-making burdens greater than earlier generations had to sort through.

Column A imposes the limits within which you have to live. Fate has decreed that you are five-foot-two, so the NBA is unlikely to come calling. Your mother was alcoholic long before you were born, and you can't rewrite your bottle-strewn childhood. The economy just tanked, so jobs are harder to come by. Rents are exorbitant, so that cute little apartment on the waterfront isn't in reach of a barista's salary. Some of these factors may affect everyone (all your friends bathe in the same economy). Others are particular to you (you're the only one you know missing a leg).

Column B covers all the factors that are at least theoretically under your control. It may take a lot of motivation to exercise, or apply for a dozen jobs, or move to Sheffield, or learn macramé, or quit drinking Goldschläger shots every night, but other people have done it and supposedly you could too.

Column B also includes the way you react to all the items in Column A.

- You may not be able to stop climate change, but you can shrink your own CO_2 footprint rather than just sinking into despair.

- You can't unelect your country's current leadership, but you can register to vote and work for a party you like better.

- You can't detoxify social media, but you can limit your own contributions to the muck.

- Maybe you can't rise from your wheelchair, but you can get yourself out of the house and not be defined by your furniture.

These shifts may not feel possible, necessarily, and you probably can't turn your reaction around in an instant. But people vary in how they respond to challenges, and much of that variation is at least theoretically available to you.

Let's take Column A as a given. Yes, there are factors that you can't change. You don't have the option of switching birth families, reworking the past, raising the dead, installing John Oliver as pope, not having diabetes, or living on Moon Base Alpha. These are the parentheses between which you live. The distance between them, however, is almost certainly greater than you think, offering you a playing field easily large enough for a life.

Also, thousands discover that factors they thought were Column A were actually Column B in drag. Maybe, despite your doubts, you *can* live in Rio, you *don't* have a brain disorder, you *aren't* hopeless at sports, and people *will* hire you.

I am constantly struck by how many of my clients see doors as hopelessly barred against them when they are actually wide open, with a welcome sign swinging in the breeze. "Oh no, I could never be an actor / write a book / go back to school / cycle Peru / run for office / move away / learn to drive / recover from my sister's death / form a relationship / give up pot / sponsor a refugee / confront my abuser / marry my same-sex partner / teach at university." Column B is bigger than most of us think. We are sometimes motivated to assign our dreams to Column A just to shut them up. We confuse the unlikely—or complicated, or difficult—with the impossible.

The trick, then, is to find the B-side elements of a good life within the A-side brackets that life has given us, and to assess and reassess the brackets themselves, to see whether they still hold. You will always have multiple risk factors for misery in your life. This is the nature of existence. We want to identify the doors that move when pushed and the locks that can be picked.

To do this, we'll look downhill. If the twenties seem so hard to perfect, we'll choose an easier task. Let's set our course for disaster, Mr. Sulu, and see what happens. If we wanted it all to go wrong, just how would we do it?

MISERY: THE FOURFOLD PATH

In Formula One racing, the trickiest parts of the track are at the tightest curves. The decade of the twenties involves sharp twists and changes of direction, helpfully providing rich opportunities to fly in flames off the course. In this book, I'll emphasize many of the deepest potholes you can steer toward.

But there's a bonus. It's not just the curves that can get you. A structural failure could occur at any time. A rival driver can cut you off. An accident ahead can leave you with nowhere to go. These can happen on the straightaways, and they can happen on the curves too. I reviewed many of these more universal routes to unhappiness in my previous book *How to Be Miserable: 40 Strategies You Already Use.* I won't pad this guide with needless repetition. Where appropriate, though, I will mention strategies that appear in that book—especially when the challenges of early adulthood offer a particular potency or a variation.

I have promised a downward path. In fact, I'll deliver four of them. Each is a superhighway, with particular challenges, signage, and detours along the way.

First, in Fight the Future, we'll take a look at the transition to adulthood itself. It may appear from a distance to be a simple on-ramp. In reality, the construction is poor, the pavement crumbles, and there are wreck-filled chasms along the way. We'll find the exits into all the worst neighborhoods.

Next, in Santa Wasn't the Only Lie, we consider how our culture makes the transition more difficult than necessary by giving us a faulty map that misrepresents the nature of adult life, substituting distorted myths for the reality of the road ahead. To feel worse, all you need to do is snap your heels together and believe, believe, believe.

In Creating a Self we look at the tricky issue of character, and how we manufacture the person we become. We'll explore faulty engineering, cracked foundations, leaky roofs, and how to install an extremely low ceiling.

Finally, in Navigating the Seas of Adulthood, we'll pull apart the console and rewire the GPS, looking at how to chart a route to unhappiness.

Ready?

No need to turn on the ignition. Just pop it into neutral and let's start coasting downhill.

PART ONE

Fight the Future— Preventing Childhood's End

We are accustomed to repeating the cliché, and to believing, that "our most precious resource is our children." But we have plenty of children to go around, God knows, and as with Doritos, we can always make more. The true scarcity we face is practicing adults.

—Michael Chabon, *Manhood for Amateurs*

When I was eleven I found a book in the school library: a guide to the West Coast Trail, a forty-seven-mile former lifesaving track established in 1907 to help rescuers access the "Graveyard of the Pacific." I resolved that when I was older I would hike this route. When I was older, I did.

The trail follows beaches and bluffs through rainforest cut with deep ravines where runoff splashes endlessly to the sea. Most of these bluffs are negotiated with a series of ancient ladders hammered into the rock. You come to a ravine, pick your way down ladder after ladder with your fifty-pound pack, cross the creek, and haul yourself up the far side. Some of the creeks have bridges. Some have slippery, moss-covered stepping-stones. A few are crossed by single logs felled across the gap, chainsawed along the top to provide some purchase. All of this in a mossy region that gets almost ten feet of rain annually.

I experienced a sinking feeling when I approached the first of these log crossings. The drop was perhaps fifteen feet, to a creek racing over large rocks. I inched my way over, conscious of the weight of my pack, holding on to an overhanging branch as long as I could. Was it really possible to let go and cross without falling? My next campsite was on the far side, but at that moment the one behind me seemed more appealing. Maybe I'd done enough for the day.

But my companions were already across and the car was at the far end, days ahead. I released the branch, fixed my gaze on the far side, and felt a surge of relief when I reached the next ladder. There were more challenges ahead, but I'd safely passed this one.

The passages of life are similar to those on the trail. Some are easy, some are tricky, and some make you long to head back and huddle in your sleeping bag. Unfortunately, giving in would only put off the inevitable. There's no way home from the trail-head, and your next meal is on the other side. Stalling creates only short-term relief—followed, as usual, by longer-term desperation.

This makes the path to misery quite simple: Just stay where you are. Flatly refuse to cross the gorge. Stretch out your child-hood as long as you possibly can. You can manage it one more year, at least, and maybe another year beyond that. The trail will always be there, though perhaps tomorrow it will be wetter and the ravine darker. Your companions on the journey will have gone on ahead, leaving you to negotiate it alone, neither more equipped nor rested than you were before.

How best to fight the future? Let's consider ten ways.

Let Parents Be Parents

Our first strategy is simplicity itself: just keep your mouth shut and don't change anything. Maybe no one will notice that the odometer has clicked over and, chronologically at least, you have become an adult.

There are tremendous advantages to prolonging childhood for as long as possible. It is, for most people, a safe harbor. And think of the bonuses:

- Your childhood home is probably bigger and better equipped than the dingy basement apartments most people get when they first move out.

- Rent, heat, light, water, and garbage removal are extremely well priced at zero dollars.

- Most meals are provided. It's like a college dorm room plan, but with fewer annoying roommates.

- Chauffeur and maid services are often tacked on at no additional charge.

How can you beat that? The demands are few and the benefits are too many to count. Why wouldn't you want that deal to continue?

The main problem with this gambit is that it depends on your parent(s) neglecting to realize that they no longer have a child on their hands. In some families this is not so great a challenge as it might seem.

- Parents' sense of their offspring's age usually lags, as you may have noticed. It's as though their image of you is the moving average of all the ages you've been since birth, so at fourteen they treat you like you were seven, and at twenty-four like you're twelve. Clean the pubic hairs off the toilet seat and they might never twig that you are post-adolescent.

- People are busy with their own lives. They barely see themselves in a mirror, so if you keep your head down they'll surely never notice you. Or your tats.

- It's great to feel needed. One of life's nagging questions is "What is my purpose?" If you have a child who can't pour cereal without supervision, you don't have to face this quandary. Your purpose is to buy their underwear, change the light bulbs, and prevent vacuuming injuries.

- Most parents are ambivalent about releasing their children into the wide, dangerous world, so they have a motive for believing you are nowhere near ready. Some of this comes from insecurity. They didn't really know what they were doing when they raised you, so there's always some late patching up to do before they can declare you "finished."

But, but, but: how is this a path to misery?

In Richard Adams's novel *Watership Down*, a group of rabbits escaping the imminent destruction of their hilltop home encounters a new warren where all seems well. The tunnels are wide, plentiful food is mysteriously delivered, and all basic needs are covered. The cost, they soon discover, is that the farmer supplying the food harvests the rabbits for meat. There's sometimes a high price to pay for security.

It's unlikely that your family are going to turn out to be cannibals fattening you up for stew. Nevertheless, the downsides are real.

- Even if you don't share it already, their sense that you can't manage your own life will tend to rub off on you. You will become as convinced as they are that you cannot make it on your own.

- Worse, that perception of helplessness will be valid, because their care will prevent you from learning the skills required. This competence deficit will only grow, given that the skill set expected of adults expands with time.

- The room service comes with an advice function that, unlike Siri or Alexa, cannot be switched off. Your ever-present Greek chorus will forever sing *"Why don't you (fill in the blank)"* in infinite variations.

- Sooner or later you'll want to make use of your romantic inclinations, and shushing your partner's cries of ecstasy so they don't wake Mom is unlikely to add points to your performance.

- You'll never really know when the oven timer will chirp and they'll declare that time is up and you have to be out by sundown.

- You will stand forever, like a tourist at a coin-operated telescope, watching your friends and peers vanish in the distance.

This strategy isn't available to everyone. Some people at the cusp of adult life have no one helping out. Or their parents have been counting the candles on the cake and withdrawing services year by year. You may be in this group. If so, then this friendly, fleece-covered trap will not fit your ankle. You'll have to find another way to derail the decade.

If, however, you are blessed with unobservant parents who have never noticed that you have opposable thumbs and can, therefore, do things for yourself, then a comfortable avenue to discomfort stretches invitingly before you. Keep quiet and allow them to continue seeing you as a child.

If they show signs of awareness that your abilities outstrip your achievements, profess your incapacity. Prove it, if necessary. Foul up any task they set before you. Spill the paint, dent the car, burn spaghetti, mow the dog, lose the McJob, and prove your inability to set an alarm clock. Wear them down. Sooner or later, they won't ask any more. The road to hell is paved with your Luke Skywalker bedsheets.

Keep Your Parents in the Pantheon

Why does virtually every culture invent religion?

Maybe one or another of the gods is real and their worshippers see things accurately. Even if that were true, though, it doesn't explain the other ten thousand divinities that we've dreamt up—all of those warring, diverse, and mutually inconsistent Asgards and Olympi.

Surely the answer is that we believe in gods because we have lived among them.

We are born into a world surrounded by comparative giants who can perform miracles. Our parents and other elders stand upright, communicate using sound, control our comfort, feed us (sometimes from their own bodies!), drive huge machines, and reveal the names and functions of all the things around us. It is from them that we receive the first Word, and every Word after that. They are masters of fire, of light, of bathwater, of life itself. They provide, and they take away. We are held in the lap of Parvati; we ride on the shoulders of Apollo.

This is a pretty great life. Don't give it up without a fight.

It gets more difficult with time, though. We long to believe that our gods are benevolent, just, and all-powerful. It is inconceivable that they lack control over their own behavior, and too frightening to imagine that they are unjust or malicious. If they seem inconsistent, or rude, or harsh, it must be that we somehow provoked them and deserve our pain. Dad yelled, so you must have done something wrong. Mom became ill, so it must be your fault. Their failings and weaknesses become your own. They leave, they hit, they cry, they die: you can use all of it as evidence of your own worthlessness.

We try to block it out, but as we get older we realize that our gods are unreliable. They make mistakes. They disclose stunning limits to their powers.

- "I don't know how to drive a standard, honey."

- "We can't afford to get you that bike this year."

- "I can't get home in time for your soccer game."

They can produce money, but not limitless amounts of it. They can be present, but not always. They can bandage wounds, but not prevent them. They are not as great as you thought. You have been duped. Swindled.

Maybe it's no surprise that out of sheer nostalgia we invent gods more powerful than the weaklings we had been worshipping—nor that we call them Heavenly Parent. Like cathedrals constructed atop Roman ruins, we create deities from the rubble of our illusions.

In the movie *On Golden Pond*, elderly Katharine Hepburn and Henry Fonda are facing their mortality and failing health. Their daughter Chelsea, played by Jane Fonda, is filled with resentment for her parents' faults. She is particularly critical of her father, whose early signs of dementia she has failed to notice. Her mother clearly has waited many years for her to realize that her parents are only human, and could never have been the perfect beings she always wanted. Eventually the mother is pushed to her limit and angrily snaps at her daughter, "Life marches on, Chels. I suggest you get on with it."

It sounds warmly reassuring to live in a world with living, walking gods in the next room. They provide a useful target for our rage: that they were not quite good enough, that they failed us the night of the prom, that they yelled when we torched the garage (it was an *accident*), that they forbade us from going on the school camping trip, that they once struck us in anger, that they missed the recital, that they let us waste our childhood in front of the television, that they went on vacation without us, that they denied us the clothes we truly wanted, that they were never financially stable, that they moved us to another city just when we were finally fitting in. That they drank. That they divorced. We can lick our wounds of self-righteousness forever, the injured party in a lawsuit that can never be resolved.

Moving on sounds easier. But this runs the risk of communicating a message you should rebel against sending. *It wasn't so bad. You didn't hurt me so much. Your torpedoes glanced off my hull. I wasn't so disappointed that I couldn't cope. You can forgive yourselves for everything, because I survived and have gone on to build a happy life.*

If we do that, we relinquish the chance to bring out our trump card: You see what you've done to me? I am your life's biggest project, and you have botched it. We take the cherished ace of our failure and drop it on the discard pile.

So, no. Become the embodiment of their damage. Make your life an accusatory billboard advertising the failings of your parents. Don't just tell them how much they hurt you. *Show* them. Remain stuck, unable and unwilling to move forward. To twist the knife deeper, manifest their failings in your own life. If they drank, drink. If they used, use. If they were unreliable, be unreliable. If they raged, rage on. Make it a family tradition. Trap them in a Catch-22: if they point out your behavior, you can brush it aside as nothing more than a pale imitation of their own. Parents who live in glass houses shouldn't throw stones.

Well-meaning friends and ill-trained therapists may tell you, "They were just doing their best."

Well, probably not. When have you ever managed to do your best for a whole day, let alone twenty years? None of us can muster our best for long. Not you, not your parents. There were failings, there was neglect, and there were foreseeable injuries, psychological or otherwise. They could have canceled the business trip, bought you that car, kept the rich partner, dumped the junkie, had that tumor checked earlier, pulled you from school, supported your dreams, and rewritten your résumé. And they didn't.

Pin that resentment to your chest. It's your war medal. Make it your identity.

Refuse the Burdens of Adulthood

What if keeping your head low and your mouth shut doesn't work? What if people around you start making demands anyway? Simple. Just turn them down.

Adulthood is overwhelming. You need to eat several times a day. You need a place to live. You need sheets, blankets, comforters. You need clothes to keep you warm. You need transportation, amusement, a way to communicate over long distances. Most of all, you need the medium of exchange that gets you all the rest: money.

Try a thought experiment. Snap your fingers and create a brand-new human before your eyes. Hand them a list of everything they need to do in order to survive. Eat, poop, pee, brush teeth, sleep on a regular schedule, clean up, do laundry, hunt and gather, and sell most of their waking hours in exchange for the sacred paper with the dollar signs on it. Watch their reaction.

"You're kidding. This stuff'll take me all day, and a lot of it will take years! Listen, sweetheart: You made me. Your mess, your job. I'll just wait over here with the cat. I didn't ask to be born, you know. When's lunch?"

Follow their lead. It's just as true for you as for your imaginary friend. You didn't sign up for this gig. No one asked if you wanted a ticket to planet Earth. Your existence is the product of your parents' lust. They decided to mess around that night and conceive you, or paid thousands to be inseminated, or failed to take precautions to ensure that you didn't exist, or opted not to terminate the pregnancy, or picked you out of the adoption lineup. Surely this makes your life, your needs, and your care *their problem*. Adopt this stance and you can offload all responsibility for your own life.

To make this gambit fly, you have to skip past a few inconvenient truths. Like what? Well, it's always hard to forget ideas once you've read them in black and white, so I'll be brief. Skim these quickly, then tear this page out of the book and flush it.

- No one else signed the waiver either. Not your parents, not your siblings, not Beyoncé. No one in all of history requested to be born, at least as far as we can tell. If you have to sign the contract to get the responsibility, then there isn't a person on Earth who's in charge of their own welfare. It ain't just you.

- Likewise, no one asked to be born into their particular body or life circumstances. We didn't ask to be male, or female, or trans, or straight, or gay, or white, or brown, or black, or rich, or impoverished, or Serbian, or deaf, or blond. We didn't ask to be born into an intact or divorced family, to religious or atheist parents, to a life of privilege or a life of struggle, to an upbringing and community of peace or one of daily bombings.

- Your family didn't sign up for you either, unless you were adopted. Even then, they didn't know who you would be, or how you might turn out. At best, they chose to have a child, or not to get in the way of one already impending, and they understood they were getting the luck of the draw.

- No one signed up to be caregivers forever. Your folks likely anticipated that they'd be on the hook for maybe three years of diapers and twenty years of parenting, and then you would be successfully launched out into the world. They can choose to extend the offer, but that's up to them. You don't get to forge their signature to make it a life sentence.

You see the problem. The whole "not my job" thing only hangs together if you don't think about it too hard—and if the people you're selling it to don't look very closely either.

This refusal to take the wheel of your own car provides two roads to misery, not just one.

First, parents may simply decline the job. They can refuse to provide assistance and support in the way you would like. This will feed your rage, disappointment, and frustration that they are not doing more. And because you're attempting to control the uncontrollable—someone else's behavior—the frustration will go on as long as you keep trying.

The other possibility is that you succeed. Your family, believing that they are responsible for you for as long as you want them to be, continue supporting you indefinitely and enable you to remain stuck. Catered meals, free accommodation, an allowance, and a complete lack of expectation or demand. All of these can seem like wins. But childhood ends partly because it gets dull after a while and our peers move on, leaving us in an ever-depopulating playroom with none of the perks of adulthood.

So this gambit is a perfect win-win if misery is your goal, or a lose-lose otherwise. And rather than fading with time, this one just gets worse the longer you work it. Eventually parents wake up and see the logical flaw in the argument, or they can't afford to keep feeding you, or they need more care themselves than they can dish out, or they take their final breath and leave the planet altogether. One way or another, there's a time limit when you're making other people steer. The path goes downhill, and downhill, and downhill—until one day it drops off a cliff.

Be a Rebel and Party On

Okay, so maybe childhood isn't worth keeping on life support. Done that, got the bib. What's next?

When you're a kid the mission is easy: you learn to follow instructions. The task of adolescence is to morph from obedient child into your own person—and how do you do that? The most logical answer is to reverse the directive. If formerly the thing to do was obey, then now the answer is to disobey. Identify what people in your life want, and do the opposite.

There are three ways that this leads to misery.

- First, it plunks you back into childhood. During the teen years, parents often want us to grow up and become responsible. Doing the opposite means rebelling against those pressures—by retaining precisely the personal qualities that we need to jettison.

- Second, it's hard to be sensibly selective about the rebellion. Some of the boundaries they advocate are actually good ideas. Heroin makes for a bad experiment, unsafe sex can have lasting consequences (both venereal and conceptual), impulsive driving kills off more of the young adult gene pool than anything else, and unbridled hostility makes other people as miserable as it does you.

• Third, it keeps us under their control, rather than freeing us. Far from asserting our independence, our behavior during a rebellion remains determined by the dictates of others. What governs whether we head out on a Tuesday-night binge with our latent-addict friends? Whether someone else disapproves, not whether we actually think it's a fun idea.

Whether our actions are chosen to conform to or contrast with others' wishes, the ultimate determinant is the outside force from which we are attempting to distinguish ourselves. Maybe we'd just as soon sit home and study, or try out a chicken poblano recipe, or go out job-hunting—but that would only hand an apparent victory to the people trying to push us in those directions.

I was always confused by Shakespeare's *Romeo and Juliet*. Romeo starts the play besotted by Rosaline, then forgets all about her the moment he sees Juliet. What was the point of that? It took a Shakespeare scholar to get me to understand the obvious message: Romeo is an idiot. The first half of the play is a comedy about hapless morons caught up in transitory puppy love. The second half is a tragedy brought about by the disapproval of the parents. Their opposition to the relationship is what makes the young rebels more disastrously determined.

The beauty of Shakespeare is in the universality of his stories. This sixteenth-century plot seems remote when first encountered. It explains an enormous number of short-lived first marriages, however, from which mutual poisoning would be a happy relief. What do you call a young man you forbid your daughter to see? A son-in-law.

And it's not just marriage. Ask your peers about any number of ill-advised life moves.

"What were you thinking?"

"I didn't want to be controlled by people telling me not to," they'll often answer.

A case in point is the aging party animal, frustrated by the gradual departure of his (or her) drinking buddies. Every bar has at least one. He's not the cool older guy who occasionally swings by old haunts. He's the one in the corner who has become part of the furniture.

In the movie *The World's End*, forty-something Gary (played by Simon Pegg) reconvenes his high school buddies in an attempt to reach the end of a twelve-stop pub crawl that they failed to complete as youth. Gary has never grown up. He's living much the same life he did in school—the manic rebel chasing the excitement of the moment and never quite reaching it.

His friends have, arguably, grown up just a little too much. They are bored with their lives and have tipped the scales on the side of sterile conformity just as much as Gary has with impulsivity. The townspeople, they discover, have been replaced with responsible robots by an exasperated race of aliens intent on taming humanity's self-destructive tendencies, as exemplified by Gary. It isn't until death is looming that Gary confesses to his mates (spoiler alert!) that his life hasn't been all that much fun, and that he is on the lam from his residential twelve-step program.

The goal should not be to retire at the age of twenty-five to *Jeopardy*, antacids, and a lawnmower. But if your desires are precisely the same as they were ten years ago, it's possible that something has gotten stuck. There are few things more lonely than the end of a party when everyone has gone home but you. For misery, stay and finish up the leftover drinks. Otherwise, learn when to call a cab and switch off the lights.

Stay on the Breast

A client of mine was mourning the departure of her son to university. She was simultaneously proud of the job she had done raising him and worried about how he would cope without her.

"When I was a child I had nothing. I swore if I had children they wouldn't suffer the way I did. He had new clothes. He was never hungry. I took the best care of him." She knew he'd have to do his own laundry. This was a concern. "He's never touched a washing machine. He won't know how."

Too late now, I thought. I elected not to challenge her on her child-raising. Her son would have a lot of catching up to do in the next few years. Like many parents, she had kept the little darling safe, fed, clothed, wiped, and burped. But she hadn't spent much time preparing him to live independently. She had indeed raised a child—but his life was increasingly demanding that he be an adult instead. By keeping him happy she had started him down a reliable road to misery.

Parenting has two central and opposing missions, balanced on a fulcrum like a teeter-totter. One task is to keep your offspring safe and protected; the other is to prepare them for your own death. Nurturance and independence. Keep the kids from the tiger, while simultaneously giving them the skills to survive if it gets you instead. Many of us got a stronger dose of one or the other. Often we get the care, without the skills.

When we're born, we're dependent on the bottle or the breast. But the breast doesn't just supply milk. It washes clothes, vacuums, makes beds, dispenses money, makes decisions for us, takes us to the pediatrician, houses us, and checks our geography homework. It's male and female. Parental and fraternal. Familial and governmental.

From the first snip of the umbilical cord, the world tries to wean us away. First they take the milk dispenser, then the diaper service, the maid service, the chef service, the chauffeur service, and, if we're not careful, even the Bank of Mom and Dad. The nurturance end of the seesaw is whittled away until we come crashing to the ground. The breast vanishes, turns the corner, goes off on ski holidays, takes night-school courses, and asks when we're going to help cook dinner.

This you should resist. Life is tough enough. Imagine independence as a path from obstetric ward to condo. You may have no choice about some of it, or you might only wake up to the problem when you've already been pushed halfway. Wherever you are, apply the brakes. Dig in your heels. Go no further.

To some extent, of course, all of us are dependent throughout our lives: on electricity, on supermarkets, on a fire department to step in if the cooking goes badly. Maximize this. Avoid learning to boil water, remove red wine stains, change a tire, or hang pictures. If the original nipple has been withdrawn, replace it with one from Ronald McDonald, Martha Stewart, or Chef Boyardee. Don't look for romantic partners; what you need are new parents.

To be truly miserable, remain helpless and dependent on others for all of your needs. There will always be an element of uncertainty in their care. Maybe no one will know how to turn on the dorm washing machines. They may not tell you to change the oil in your car. They may neglect to wake you up in the morning, or make you write thank you emails, or iron your dress shirt for the job interview. The only way out of the trap is to know how to take care of yourself. If you don't, you're stuck there for life.

Relying on others doesn't work for everyone. Some people in their twenties have no one to pick up the slack. The family is gone, or unsupportive—or prioritizes building capacity over fostering dependence. These individuals have no choice but to make their own way. If they want to be miserable, they'll have to find another route.

Many, however, are provided with more nurturance than they need. Some parents enmesh love and caregiving so thoroughly that they can't see the difference. Cleaning up after their children, making their food, and buying their clothes are acts of love. Not to do these things would be neglect, or an affirmation that they don't really care all that much. So they keep on cooking.

Some families claim to support their offspring's independence, but harbor a contrary motive hidden even from them. They secretly fear being abandoned by a young person who does not need them anymore. So they never pull back, weighting down the nurturance end of the seesaw and stranding their young adult in midair.

Think of the supports that you might be getting from family—the various breasts pointed your way. One path is to continue accepting these for as long as they are offered, and to avoid learning how to cope without them until absolutely necessary. At that point you will be in a panic to learn. You'll be unequipped for the road ahead.

Also, you will always be irritated by their help, even though you're the one seeking it out. Every favor they grant, every need they fulfill, will be a frustrating reminder of your own incapacity, and their infuriating superiority.

The alternative would be to begin giving up benefits voluntarily, without waiting for them to be withdrawn. Take transit rather than waiting for the ride. Do your own laundry rather than tossing it in the communal hamper. Make your own meals, or join in the rotation of people making food for the household. Budget, so that you can make do without the strings-attached loans. Look long and hard at that tempting breast. And turn away. At some point in your life, it will be time for solid food.

LESSON 6

Wait for Permission

Maybe you feel the urge to build your life, but no one is prodding you into it. No familial pirate is jabbing you out along the gangplank. It's still hard to decide when to take the leap. When are you ready to travel on your own, stay overnight with a romantic interest, move away, opt out of the family religion, choose your own career, or decide whom to marry?

One option: when your parents say so. This has been true all your life. They have established themselves as the ultimate authority—the arbiter of all decisions about your appropriate level of independence. So why doubt them now? To be miserable, just keep them in the role they already occupy.

A young woman attending a local university came to see me, dissatisfied with her life. She'd lost all enthusiasm and interest for her courses. Everything just seemed blah. When I asked what she did all day, I could see why. Although she said she had friends, she seldom saw them, or did much of anything outside of school. She talked about the strained relationship she had with her mother, and that it was especially aggravating in the car when she was being driven to university.

Hold up, I thought. *Being driven to school? At twenty-three?*

I asked her why she didn't see her friends more often. Most of them would only have been a short transit ride away. Her answer: "I'm not allowed to take the bus." Her parents had forbidden public transit. If she wanted to go somewhere, Mom or Dad had to drive her. She'd signed up for driving lessons a year or two earlier, but somehow it never proved quite the right time to get started, or for her parents to help her learn.

Startled, I let slip the first thing that came into my head. "You're allowed to vote. You're allowed to drink. You're allowed to fight in the Armed Forces."

Sometimes bluntness helps, sometimes not. This time? Not so much. But it did open up the subject of her parents' fears for her safety, and their apparent ambivalence about her independence.

In 1990, poet Robert Bly published *Iron John*, a book that became a touchstone for the new age men's movement of the time. In it, he retells the Grimms' fairy tale of the same name. Though pitched for a male protagonist, the point is universal. I'll paraphrase it.

A king captures a wild man of the forest and imprisons him in a cage in the castle courtyard. A golden ball, favorite toy of the king's young son, rolls into the cage. The wild man agrees to give it back, but only on the condition that the boy unlocks the door. Terrified, the boy runs away.

Years pass. Eventually the boy, now grown up, returns, still seeking the golden ball. He talks to the wild man, who reveals that the key is hidden under the queen's pillow. It's clear that the boy's mother won't give it up voluntarily. He must steal it, and he does. He opens the cage and, fearing the reaction of his parents, runs off with the wild man into the forest.

The story continues, but the significant point for our purpose has been reached: the key must be stolen and, once it is, childhood is over.

At the risk of overexplaining the obvious, the wild man of the story represents the boy's adult self, caged by his parents' fear of his independence. He can ask for the key, but his parents, anxious about his safety and their own abandonment, will not give it to him voluntarily. To become an adult, he must not wait for Mom and Dad to hand over his freedom like some kind of belated Bar Mitzvah gift. Ultimately, the key must be taken, as it will not be bestowed.

So…is this just a guy thing? Hardly. Even more well-known is the Grimm story of long-haired Rapunzel, who is imprisoned by her mother, a witch, high in a doorless tower. She welcomes the visits of a young suitor who climbs her hair, and has him bring a scrap of cloth each time so she can weave an escape ladder. The witch foils the plan, blinds the prince, and sends her now-pregnant daughter into exile, but eventually Rapunzel prevails and is reunited with her date.

Once again, a parent figure attempts to prevent the autonomy of a maturing child, who hatches a plan to escape rather than securing permission. The stranger (a remarkably ineffectual prince this time, rather than a wild man) can't effect the rescue solo. Rapunzel has to take the initiative, and though she fails at first, she ultimately wins.

These tales paint a fairly discouraging portrait of family life, one in which parents aren't exactly fostering their offspring's independence. But they make the point that my transit-challenged client needed to learn: her parents might never gift-wrap her adulthood and hand it to her. At some point she would need to give herself permission to live as the adult that she already was.

We don't need to toss our parents onto the trash heap of personal history and march off into the woods with every hairy potential molester that comes along. But we should be wary of the pitfalls of waiting until our parents—fearful for our safety and uncertain about the job they have done preparing us—declare us "ready" to make steps in our lives that we will only truly be ready for once we have made them.

The alternative is to wait, combing our hair in a prison tower of our family's making, trapped in a stagnating childhood, prevented from learning about the world and waiting to be judged knowledgeable enough to enter it. The boy does not unlock the wild man's cage fearlessly. He trembles, unsure whether he is doing the right thing. We will never feel entirely ready, and those around us will never believe we are, until we have done it.

The message is clear: For misery, wait endlessly until those who have had power over you say you are ready. For adulthood, steal the key and open the door to the outside world.

Change Your Family, Not Yourself

So there you are: parachute on, standing in the windy doorway of the airplane, ready to jump. Or, no. Not quite ready. You'd like just a little more time to think about it. How can we slow all this down?

Easy. Impose a prerequisite. Demand that other people change before you take over the controls of your life. This gives you the perfect justification to sit back and wait, possibly forever.

In early adulthood, almost everyone uses this strategy to some extent. Our parents, our siblings, our teachers, our bosses— someone else needs to change and then things will go great. So dig in. Make it your life's mission to have them show some consideration, change their religion, lose weight, leave each other, get back together, see your value, exercise, vote your way, lower the toilet seat, raise the toilet seat, move to a better part of town, get to work, retire, apologize for the way they treated you when you were nine, or agree that the path you have chosen is the right one and cheer from the sidelines.

Years ago I wrote a guide to effective communication (*The Assertiveness Workbook*). Ever since, time-pressured interviewers have asked me to state the single core concept of assertiveness. For the longest time, this question would stump me. The book is essentially two hundred pages of tips. I had no clue which one was the Jenga block without which the whole thing would fall apart.

With time, though, I came to see one idea as more important than all the others: assertiveness is about giving up on trying to control other people, and controlling ourselves instead. This reflects a harsh reality. The only person we really have control over is us. The feeling of helplessness that overtakes us when we try to control others is valid. We *are* helpless. They may change because of something that we do, but it will be because we changed ourselves, not them.

One way to avoid moving forward in life is to concentrate your efforts on the doors that are firmly locked against you. This way you can feel like you are doing something while accomplishing nothing useful. One of the best projects for this is reforming the behavior of the people around you. You'll have more success if you push for changes that meet two criteria:

1. They are at least theoretically possible (there's nothing stopping Mom from taking a defensive driving course).

2. The benefits, if the change were to come about, would genuinely be significant (your sister really would be better off without that loser husband).

Your parents (and the rest of your family) are perhaps the people you know best in all the world. You see them up close for extended periods, and you know the challenges and barriers in their lives. From the vantage point of an intimate observer, you can see how things could change for the better with only a few simple shifts. If Dad would just quit drinking, if your stepsister would just take her meds, if your brother would handle his finances just a little more responsibly. The tweak seems so small, the need so obvious.

Often the change involves how they interact with you. If Mom were only a tad more generous, you could afford a better school. If Dad would only acknowledge your true value, you could relax and begin to feel it yourself. If your brother would just apologize for how he treated you last summer, you could put it behind you. And it's not as though such wishes are unrealistic or unjust. The imperfections are real. Feelings were hurt. Mistakes were made.

Focusing on the reform of others is a road to misery precisely because that door is latched from the inside. You will keep banging fruitlessly on the knocker forever.

The futility of this strategy is easy to miss partly because it cunningly hides the reality. Standing up for yourself and demanding change can feel like an act of individuality and self-direction. It shows how you, the newly minted adult, have developed your own perspective and plan to put it into action.

Unfortunately, this places ultimate control in the hands of others. *They* get to decide whether or not to change, whereas you are simply the petitioner. You can plead, argue, and prove your point endlessly and they never really have to change at all. Pushing harder against their resistance almost always steels their resolve, so the more pressure you bring to bear, the less likely you are to produce the effect you desire.

But wait, you might argue. What's the alternative when the people you love don't agree with your life, or cancel out your vote with their own, or hold you back by failing to give the right kind of support, or damage their own lives with their misguided actions? Your only option is to keep shoving, no?

Good. Stick to that reasoning. It'll never pay off, but it will keep you stuck, make you miserable, and prevent you from taking charge of your own life.

Of course, there is an alternative. You could give up on changing your relatives. You could regard this declaration of defeat, as many therapists do, as a central developmental task. In order to move on, you may need to let them do what they do, believe what they believe, think what they think (even about you), and be who they are, like it or not. This would acknowledge and confront the limitations of your own powers.

This hands-off style wouldn't necessarily prevent you from offering your perspective. "Mom, your gambling could lose you the house." "Dad, taking up mountain unicycling at sixty is a bad idea." But you could refrain from putting your own life on hold, pending their acceptance of your advice. All of the energy that has been devoted to the struggle could be redirected to another door, perhaps one that is unlocked and waiting for you.

If that other door opened, though, you might have to step through it. Better to keep knocking on the ones that will never budge.

Shorten the Decade

On my twentieth birthday, the decade ahead looked endless. One hundred and twenty months. A month can fly by, but a decade? Impossible.

Maybe you too have seen an eternity stretch before you. You can make it shorter.

Chances are, you spend about eight hours a day asleep or in bed. That's forty months gone already; eighty months remaining. Can we shorten it more?

According to the American Time Use Survey,[9] US citizens average:

- 1.2 hours per day eating and drinking, or just over six months per decade

- 40 minutes a day for personal grooming, or about 3.5 months

- about a month each on laundry and grocery shopping

Now we're down to 68.5 months. Add a few more items. Commuting. Vacuuming. Cleaning the toilet. Looking for your keys. You've cut the decade in half without even trying.

But you know where I'm heading with this, right?

In the movie *Men in Black*, Agents K and J wipe the recent memories of people who have seen the aliens inhabiting Earth. They use what J, played by Will Smith, refers to as "the flashy thing." For my *How to Be Miserable* talks I stole this idea for a demonstration with a penlight.

"Imagine that I could erase some of your memories, but that you could identify a few that you wanted to keep. Think of one memory you'd want on that list, and nod when you have it."

Try it yourself, then read on when you have your memory in mind.

I would wait for people to give me the signal, then ask, "During that memory, raise your hand if you're looking at a computer, phone, or television." This little gambit is virtually foolproof. Two, or one, or zero people in a room of hundreds raise their hands.

To be sure, all of us have a few favorite memories from looking at screens: learning that your brother is out of the hospital, receiving an invitation to an event, seeing a wonderful movie. But the exercise demonstrates that the density of memorable experiences is considerably lower for most of us when we are gazing at screens than when we are not. The vast majority of our cherished memories occur when we are looking elsewhere.

One path to misery is to reduce the number of positive, memorable, or uplifting experiences in our lives. Shrinking the time we spend in the real world is an effective way of accomplishing this.

A recent Nielsen Company survey[10] found that the average American spends ten hours and twenty-four minutes each day looking at screens of one sort or another (computer, tablet, phone, or television). (Oh, you're not in America? Other nationalities won't be too far from this figure.) That's fifty-four months per decade. If this is added to sleep time and the other activities listed above, that shortens the non-screen decade of the twenties to 14.5 months. A little over one year. String eight one-year decades together and your life is just about over.

Let's look at it another way. In an average 79.3-year American life span, screen time alone takes up 51.5 years of waking life, shortening the real-world waking life span to 27.8 years in which to experience *everything else that life has to offer.* Love, adventure, beauty, nature, child-raising, travel—everything. Add sleep back into the equation and we have a total life span of 44.9 years spent in the analog, non-screen world—just a bit longer than the American life expectancy of 42.5 years in 1890, a span that seems shockingly brief to many of us today. Yet that's close to what we now have. By comparison, smoking only reduces the life span by about ten years[11]—and obesity by considerably less.[12]

I know—some of that screen time is at work. Most jobs involve toiling over hot computers. Sure, but much of our screen time is outside work hours.

Oh, but: You can learn French from online programs. You can read books on a tablet. You can cook while Skyping with your grandmother. It's not like you flush all that time down the toilet.

Except, well, most of us do. Internationally, users average about two hours per day on social media—the nutritionally empty aspartame of tribal life. We watch Netflix, we look at cat videos, we obsessively check the news, we tweet, we look up the actor who played Rick on *The Walking Dead.* We pass the time mostly without enriching our lives. One reason for the increased incidence of depression during the twenties may simply be that the twenties are shorter than they used to be. There is too little time for the experiences that support our mood.

An old principle of mining is "Dig where the gold is likely to be." If our goal is misery, then one way to get there is to spend the majority of our time digging where we know the nuggets of happiness are few and far between. Getting embroiled in Reddit posts. Counting our likes on Instagram. Wandering the halls of Wikipedia.

In my work and private life, I've spent a fair bit of time on palliative care wards. It's true what they say: no one, at the end of their life, says they wished they'd spent more time at work. But likewise, no one says they wished they'd spent more time watching *Game of Thrones*.

For a less happy, less engaged life—indeed, for less life overall—relentlessly immerse your consciousness in the digital world. For the reverse, you might have to reconsider your daily dose of pixels.

Or did you want happiness instead? Well, we can't just abandon the digital world altogether. I'm typing in it right now. But perhaps our choices about how to spend the only currency that really matters—our time—could be just a little bit more conscious.

The clock, after all, is ticking.

Chill

It's sometimes hard to predict whether a certain course of action will make you feel better or worse, because often it will do both. Drinking eight beers may make you feel upbeat for a while, but tomorrow you'll have a hangover. Replacing the brake pads on the car will be boring, but may result in a happier road trip. Using a condom may be a bit of a buzzkill, but not as much as next week's genital rash.

The same decision can lead to short-term cheerfulness and long-term regret, or to short-term aversion and long-term satisfaction. Pick your poison. Heedless hedonism is one of the best ways of achieving misery. Try it and see.

And why not? By twenty, you've spent well over a decade in school. You've been bullied, bossed around, unfairly accused, ridiculed, humiliated, and probably dumped. During puberty your body spent five years rebelling and your mind rode the roller coaster from hell.

Why not sit back, take a breather, and just live your life for a while? Chill out. You're in your twenties. There's plenty of time to do all that you want. There'll be time later on for school, a career, personal development, family, a purpose. You can afford to declare an intermission, relax, and enjoy the decade. You can worry about your future in your future.

Sounds good, right? But how does enjoying life lead to misery?

It doesn't have to. Depends on how you do it. Except—well, life isn't really so long. At twenty you're halfway to forty. Wait a decade to get your act together and you may experience a rising tide of panic for most of the trip there. It's like hosting a cocktail party on a gently tilting *Titanic*.

- If eventual partnership is on the agenda, you may want to keep an eye out for candidates and hold a few auditions. Waiting a decade to think about finding a mate, getting a place to live, and then possibly reproducing (if that's on the agenda) may make the timeline a bit tight. By the mid-thirties, fertility is already fading, and the seemingly limitless energy needed to parent may be approaching its best-by date.

- Most people achieving great things in their thirties do so because they laid the foundations earlier. Getting started on postsecondary education or a career at thirty can feel like running to the pool, hopping awkwardly to get a leg into your swimsuit, when everyone else is on their third lap.

- Even the short-term enjoyment may not be so great. Most people who chill through their twenties aren't any happier than those who are more productively engaged. Often the time is spent on video games (imaginary skills in an imaginary world), television (watching other people pretend to have lives), or altered states (skill-free existence that you can't remember well later). Great temptations, but not much payoff in terms of satisfaction.

Months can pass without notice, but years won't. Eventually you may wonder why you treated your youth as a form of early retirement.

I know I risk sounding like your grandfather here. "You need to settle down, young lady/man, and get over the idea that life is supposed to be fun." You should knuckle down, decline all invitations, never touch a drop, study, work long into the night, and be a model of responsibility and respectability for all to admire.

Maybe. That's another path to misery. You could take it instead. The choice between complete hedonism and utter responsibility may seem like a pretty wide fork in the road, but both arrive at the same unhappy destination.

Adulthood, as described by elders, career counselors, and books on the subject, can feel like a waterslide into drudgery— one that's hard to escape once the current has grabbed you. They often imply that life has a script, all of us are the actors, and it's up to us to play the role our culture has assigned us until the curtain comes down.

Here's how the story is supposed to go after high school:

- You achieve some form of postsecondary education targeted to a specific field.

- You catch the rung of a career ladder and start climbing.

- You buy real estate and try not to feel the mortgage as a twenty-five-year leash around your neck.

- You form romantic attachments until you find one person you can imagine spending the rest of the play with, and you marry them.

- You have children and spend the next twenty years or more raising them.

- You tough out a midlife crisis without buying a sports car or having an affair with a twenty-two-year-old, and you get used to the idea that time is passing.

- You retire, with your children off climbing their own ladders, your mortgage paid, and your prostate prodded or your pap smeared.

- Curtain! After which everyone sits for forty-five minutes at your funeral and marvels at how well you played your role and how lifelike you look.

Woo-hoo. Inspiring. There seems to be a very narrow window for self-exploration and self-expression, after which it's all pretty much prescribed. If you take a gap year, you're just putting off the inevitable.

But for people a little further down the road who claim happiness, the script may not look much like this. There are deviations aplenty, and whole acts of the play are skipped, shortened, overhauled, or revised beyond recognition. No law dictates that marriage is a requirement, you don't have to have kids if you don't want them (the last thing the world needs is more reproduction), you don't have to work a nine-to-five job, and you may never have to retire if you don't want to.

The problem is that when you finally want to adopt a longer-term outlook for your life, you may lack some critical equipment—like a degree, marketable skills, relationship savvy, or self-discipline. You may have to take another decade to build those up, by which time your peers may be fifteen or twenty years ahead of you and banks may be wondering if they can risk a mortgage on someone your age.

Perfect for misery. But what if you're one of those spoilsports looking for happiness instead?

Well, then, by all means, explore during your twenties. Try out new things. Travel. Have short-term relationships. Diversify. But don't delude yourself that life is long. It isn't. There are no months or years to kill with nothing to show for it.

The twenties are not a "throwaway decade" (as Meg Jay puts it in her book *The Defining Decade*). If you're going to explore, get something from it. Take a summer out in the woods, but learn backcountry survival, rock-climbing, kayaking—something. Go to Europe, but don't sit the whole time on the beach texting your friends back home. Work or volunteer at something that pushes your skills or boundaries. Come back with a thicker dossier of skills, not just a thinner wallet.

Never Give an Inch

On my consulting room bookshelf I have a pegboard puzzle called Bandits of the Natchez Trace. Three bandits and three sheriffs have to cross a river using a two-person boat. At no time can the sheriffs be outnumbered by the bandits, and the boat can't row itself across or back.

Ferrying the six across two at a time and having one row the boat back looks like the best option—but soon runs into the outnumbering problem. The surprisingly simple solution is at one point to take both a sheriff and a bandit back in the wrong direction. It's hard to notice because the goal of getting everyone across blinds us to it. It feels like we are losing ground. Resist this move and you're stuck in miserable stasis with a bandit's gun in your back.

Building an adult life is a relentless series of bandit problems, during which we are forced to abandon a goal in order to achieve it.

- We want more money and more freedom, so we remain penniless in school so that we can graduate.

- We want to party for a week over spring break, so we stay home and study diligently for the month beforehand.

- We want to buy a car for the joy of mobility, so we forego that joy and save our money until we have enough.

For misery, resist the setback. Refuse to make any move that leads backward, that sacrifices something you want. Insist that every step you take must improve your circumstances. Because most significant goals involve giving ground in order to take ground, you'll soon find yourself stuck.

Nowhere is this problem more extreme or vexing than when contemplating a move out of the family home.

You want comfort. You want to eat. You want to have enough money to go out with friends. You want to feel like a success, like you can stand on your own two feet. You want, most of all, your own apartment. But to get it, you have to sacrifice what little wealth you've been able to accrue on rent; to give up whatever level of support you get from family; and to make do with less space, less comfort, lesser furnishings, and likely a lousier neighborhood than you've lived in your whole life.

Some factors can make it even harder:

- Living in a city with extremely high rents and property values

- Starting out in a wealthy family, where the home you'll be leaving is particularly well-appointed

- Having a family that actually gets along, and that you'll miss when you go (in this way, a supportive family can be both curse and blessing)

- A situation in which the logical leap is a long one—from farm to city, from lifelong hometown to school on the other side of the country, from small pond to big ocean

This is no pegboard game. It's not just crossing back over an imaginary river. It's dropping about eighty points on the quality-of-life scale. You'll live in somebody's basement, or in a 300-square-foot concrete box, or in a five-story walk-up with cockroaches. Chances are, it's the biggest social-class high-dive you'll make in your entire life. Plus, factoring in wage stagnation, there's no real guarantee that you will ever again reach the level of housing and support that once was free and that you voluntarily gave up.

So be careful which doors you exit. Having it hit your butt on the way out is the least of your worries. The door may lock behind you, and you may discover that you've just said sayonara to a life on which you have become extremely dependent, and to which you can never return.

Better to just sit back. Stay home. Refuse to give ground. Becalm your life. Let those hoping to scale loftier peaks of satisfaction venture out into the wider world. For you, the molehill of home is surely high enough.

PART TWO

Santa Wasn't the Only Lie

As a child I assumed that when I reached adulthood, I would
have grown-up thoughts.

—David Sedaris, *Let's Explore Diabetes with Owls*

In my consulting room I have a variety of props that I can pull
out to illustrate situations and concepts that may apply to my
clients' lives. A wooden snake, a mirror, a set of toy cars (perfect
for describing traffic accidents), a puzzle box, a crystal ball.

One of my favorites is a cone of plasticized fabric with a hole
in the narrow tail. It looks like a baker's icing cone, but it's actually a sea anchor. Cast overboard, it acts something like a parachute, slowing a sailboat against the current. As it's all but
invisible from above, an unobservant skipper might not notice if
a duplicitous crew member deployed it to ensure that a race was
lost.

The sea anchor is a great metaphor for destructive ideas that can guide our behavior without our knowledge. Unaware, we can slog through life believing notions like "I'm incapable of relationships" or "I fail at everything I try" or even "Everyone loves me," which are dragging us off course. Discovering these beliefs and snipping away the invalid ones is at the core of cognitive therapy.

Some of our loopier ideas are taught to us directly. "You're the stupid one in the family." "No one is going to love you." "You are a bad girl." "Your mother is a conniving witch." We learn these at someone's knee, and sometimes we can hear their voice when we repeat them to ourselves.

Other principles we pick up through experience. "If you rely on someone, they will abandon you." "Men are cold and rejecting." "Nonconformity is dangerous." No one has to tell us these things. We observe them. By watching our parents bash each other's lights out, we develop the one that goes "Marriage isn't so great." By noticing that no one attends our soccer games or ballet recitals, we learn "I am unimportant."

We usually adopt these ideas automatically, without thinking about them all that much. "Gravity will probably work today" is an assumption underlying much of what we do, even though we aren't aware of holding it. "Fathers are unreliable" can be similar, if that's been our experience of the world thus far. "Planning is pointless." "Bosses are bullies."

Whether taught or experienced, most of our ideas about how the world works are true—or helpful in certain circumstances. "Don't wash your fuchsias with your whites." "People like compliments." "Studying while stoned is a waste of time." All of us, however, have some unhelpful, overblown, misapplied, or dead wrong sea anchors pulling us toward the rocks, such as "Modern cars don't need their brakes checked."

Not all of our faulty or destructive ideas are negative, nor are they imposed upon us by our enemies. Many are cheerful or inspirational mistruths sprinkled upon us by well-meaning parents, teachers, and websites. "The universe has our best interests at heart." These nicer-sounding ones can be especially difficult to jettison.

And that brings us to a treatise on human development. Forgive me while I digress for a moment.

Introductory psychology instructors are desperate for laughs. The one standard joke in the syllabus concerns the "four Fs" that the hypothalamus governs: Feeding, Fleeing, Fighting, and Mating. Hilarious.

Eager for more, many trot out Sigmund Freud as a figure of fun. One of the chief targets is the anal stage in his theory of psychological development. Mention the butt and undergraduates are guaranteed to giggle.

In fact, the anal stage isn't such a crazy concept. Until age two or three, the infant is primarily a receptive object: it gets fed and changed, and it mostly rolls around on the floor. In the anal stage, the toddler begins to exert control over its own bodily functions. By controlling or not controlling its sphincter, it influences the reactions of diaper-weary parents. Your first poop in the potty was almost certainly the greatest gift you ever gave Mom and Dad. No point in trying to top that.

For this reason, Freud thought that events that occur during the anal stage are hugely influential on future personality development. Can you please people? Can you produce on demand? Having learned to open and close your butthole, can you learn to shut your piehole as well?

There are other momentous milestones in development too, the biggest of which is realizing that your parents are liars. Their responsibility is to inform you about the world: what ducks sound like, where the fire engine is going, and whether they're going to keep the poop you labored over. Then one day you discover that they can look you in the eye and shamelessly mislead you.

For some of us, one of the biggest stunners is the revelation that there is, in fact, no Santa Claus. (Not into Christmas? Insert comparable cultural fib here.) This was the first crack in the dam, soon to be followed by many more. It was then that you learned the truth: your parents are not to be trusted. Whereas previously you could simply open wide and swallow whatever they gave you, now you need to be on guard, lest you be deceived once more. Fool me once, shame on you; fool me twice and I may end up in a UFO cult if I'm not careful.

The truth is, Santa wasn't the only lie. Nor are your parents the only liars. During development, you are virtually surrounded by Pinocchios, their lengthening noses stabbing at you like swords. You are trained in falsehoods by everyone: your parents, your teachers, your peers, your media—even your mentors and therapists. Like Santa and other myths, many of these mistruths are told to you partly out of kindness, partly out of a wish about how the world *should* be, and partly to enlist you in shoring up their own distorted view of the world.

To be truly unhappy in life, the mission is simple. Just believe what you're told.

There's an unfortunate paradox here. These ideas are easier to believe if you don't look at them too closely. Seeing them described in this chapter may inadvertently cause them to quiver, to flake at the edges, to lose a wheel or two.

So read on if you dare. But squint and skim, or the anchor lines might let go.

You Are Special

Surely there isn't a Christian in the world who hasn't wondered if, just maybe, they're the second coming of the Messiah, or a Jewish youth who didn't hope they were the first, or a Buddhist who didn't suspect they were the next Siddhartha. Every singer is Beyoncé II, every actor is the next Natalie Portman, every golfer is Tiger Junior.

It's a natural thought. Early on, you haven't figured out much about yourself, and so the full range of possibility expands outward. Maybe you're The One. Time passes and you realize, hopefully pretty quickly, that you are not the next savior or Wayne Gretzky after all—but that you can still live a good and admirable life.

Once that tip-top shelf in the aspirational bookcase has been abandoned, however, we can still entertain the idea that we are unique—and not unique in the different-but-equal sense of snowflakes, but unique and *better*. Special. Talented beyond the reach of our peers.

Persistently popular stories often contain a core of deeply resonant and recurrent themes that appeal to human psychology. C. G. Jung called these themes "archetypes." One of the most enduring archetypes in literature and cinema involves the secret legacy.

- Luke, an insignificant, orphaned moisture farmer on Tatooine, is unknowingly the heir of a powerful family and brother to a princess.

- Mia Thermopolis is a typical New York City teen-ager until Mary Poppins herself descends in a limo to reveal that she is actually Princess Mia of Genovia.

- Harry is just a lightning-scarred orphan boy living under the stairs, until he turns out to hold the key to the survival of the wizarding world.

- In many versions of the Cinderella story, our heroine is revealed to be nobility, a fact of which she had previously been unaware.

We indulge in a succession of stories in which the seemingly ordinary individual is revealed to be unique—a princess or prince in unknowing disguise.

Why is this such a recurring theme? Partly because it meshes so beautifully with our hopes: that we will succeed, that we are more than we seem. The trick to getting someone to believe something is not to prove that it's true. It's to make them *want* to believe it. We want to be special, so we are receptive to messages that suggest we are.

Specialness also reflects our genuine experience of ourselves. Of all the people on Earth, one is distinct from all the others. We hear our own thoughts, experience our emotions directly, and feel our body from the inside. We are, from our perspective (which, let's face it, is the only one we have), utterly unique. It seems unreasonable (unless we think hard about it) that this special person should be subject to the same constraints as all the others.

Current trends in parenting tend to support this distinction between self and other. We are told how special we are, how unique, and how brilliant. Even our bowel movements are cooed over. If we drop a crayon on a piece of paper we are artists. If we wade through a puddle we are Olympic-swimmers-in-waiting. If we like dinosaurs we are future Nobel winners. Being told that we are "about like the others" or "good enough, but not out-standing"? This is a deep wound. An unforgivable insult.

Why does our culture indoctrinate us in specialness? To build up the young person's self-esteem. The difficulty is that we construct this perception on a foundation of lies and artificiality. Actually, that poop is not particularly impressive, that macaroni isn't the best ever made, that finger painting isn't cubist, and that penalty kick could have been stopped by anybody. But we want to feel special, so we take the praise and hug it tight.

Which is great—if the world would continue to cooperate. But it doesn't.

- We get into an academic setting where someone informs us that we are not writing full sentences, that the exam last week was not voluntary, and that (to borrow from *The Princess Bride*), "You keep using that word; I do not think it means what you think it means."

- We get into the work world and have to obey the same rules as everyone else. Our mere presence doesn't justify our salary, and we don't get to cast off dull jobs to our inferiors the day after our hire. "At least learn where the bathrooms are before we promote you to vice president, mm-kay?"

- In friendships, we soon discover that if we don't sometimes pick up the bill, issue the invitation, listen rather than talk, and note others' birthdays, we get dropped. "If you're so great, you can at least get to my wedding on time with your hair brushed, no?"

- We finally form a romantic partnership and learn that our glowing sensuality does not make up for our messiness, inability to cook, infidelity, or tendency to voice criticisms as they occur to us. "Oh, you want a threesome? Go home with those two over there; I'm outta here."

The more our specialness is the core of our identity, the more disturbing it is when it is torn away. The temptation is to retrieve our uniqueness from the floor and reclaim it. Or to reject our peers, professors, partners, and employers as hostile morons who can't seem to see or appreciate the real us. "They just don't get me." Alternatively, we can retreat from the cruel world that cannot detect our inner value. All of these are paths into various flavors of misery: anxiety, anger, and loneliness.

The route out of misery is the unattractive option of acknowledging the truth: although we genuinely *are* unique, we are only about as unique as everyone else. The rules that apply to others apply to us; the expectations are the same as well. We are not royalty, secret or otherwise—neither wizard, nor princess, nor Jedi.

Maybe it's just as well. Special can be overrated. We might not be the Messiah (good: look what happened to Him). If we're special, it might not be in the way we want. It could be in the way Oedipus was special—a prince, abandoned as a baby and now grown up, who unknowingly kills his father, beds his mother, and eventually puts his own eyes out when he realizes what he's done.

So, hey—there are worse things than being ordinary.

You Have a Right to Unconditional Positive Regard

"Go where you are celebrated, not tolerated."

This adage, variously formulated and attributed, crops up on my social media feeds with infuriating regularity. It makes me jealous. It implies that there are people who are surrounded by friends and family who celebrate their very existence and everything they say and do. I don't know these people and I am most assuredly not one of them. Some people seem to like me, some don't. Most are indifferent. In this I resemble the vast majority of the human race.

Nevertheless, it sounds lovely to be universally celebrated. Every day an awards show, with me the blushing recipient of all the applause. What could be better than that?

In 1951 Carl Rogers published *Client-Centered Therapy*,[13] a book defining the crucial aspects of a therapist's manner. These include empathy, genuineness, and *unconditional positive regard* (or UPR)—a relatively new term that meant a stance of unfailing respect and warmth that didn't vary based on what the client said or did. They'd get UPR if they applied for a new job, overcame a fear, started taking crack again, attended late, showed up without pants, whatever.

And it's a good thing. In therapy, people benefit from being relatively free of the worry that their therapist will criticize them. As tempting as it might be to do sometimes, criticizing seldom produces positive therapeutic change. The job of a therapist is to create an open, inquiring space where all may be revealed, discussed, and analyzed.

But the important thing to remember is that therapists get *paid* to do this. We're still human. After working for months with someone addicted to gambling, we might groan internally when they announce that they're hungover from a night at the casino. We just try not to show it. That's UPR for you. It's a behavior. A technique. We've seen a lot in our careers, so we do tend to have a wider perspective and a greater acceptance of setbacks than your gym buddy. But we ain't perfect.

The thing is, no one else is paid to give us unconditional positive regard. So they don't.

Before long, the idea escaped the therapy setting. Late one night, someone in a secret government psych lab knocked over a beaker. Unconditional positive regard broke free and got out through the vents, infecting the culture at large. People began talking about it as though it were a normal part of human nature. Thus exposed, some began to expect it as a right in their relationships. *Our friends and family should love us exactly the same way and to the same degree no matter how we are or what we do. If they don't, they're violating the social contract.*

Older people tended to be immune. They'd been exposed to enough criticism and discord in relationships that they couldn't believe that anyone would ever actually act this way. Also, many of them realized that they didn't feel unconditional positive regard toward even their own children, let alone their coworkers, friends, or (God knows) spouse. Everyone who's held a screaming baby at four in the morning knows that UPR is an act at best.

As so often is the case, the vulnerable were the young. Not having been in the role of spouse or parent, they didn't have firsthand knowledge to combat the virus. And the infection kept getting introduced and reintroduced via the culture and, in many cases, via the educational system. *We should all be treated with kindness and acceptance at all times, no matter how we behave. Love that is contingent on our behavior is not really love at all.*

A belief in unconditional positive regard creates an expectation that people's attitude toward us will remain the same no matter what we do. Forget their dinner party, show up late, ignore their texts, insult their jobs, vomit on their carpet? Shouldn't matter. When it does, those people are violating the code of social responsibility, and our only reasonable response is rage and disappointment. By not having the social awareness to exhibit UPR, they open themselves up to punishment and abandonment.

The trick is to do all this without noticing four tiny facts:

1. We don't actually have unconditional positive regard for others. When a friend disses our new haircut or a teaching assistant trashes our research report, we feel a bit differently toward them for a while. So it's unlikely that others can manage it toward us.

2. Our anger at people's failure to support us unconditionally is, in itself, a failure of unconditional positive regard on our part.

3. Saying "Oh, but it's their behavior I reject, not them" is almost always self-deluding nitpickery. We may think we hate the sin and not the sinner, but it's the sinner we dwell on.

4. Expecting others to exhibit what we ourselves cannot manage to muster is narcissism, not fairness. "How come I have to give this to you and you don't have to give it to me?"

If you can avoid these four inconvenient truths, your course is set for misery. You have an ideal tool with which to bludgeon everyone around you: "You're not treating me unconditionally!"

Just don't look too closely. If you start to believe that you're hitting them with a myth, your weapon will dissolve into smoke before your eyes.

Happiness Is Stupid

Earlier I pointed out that in developed economies most people have things pretty good, and I feigned slight surprise at people's ability to be unhappy. But what if misery is the only logical or morally defensible course, not just one option among several? What if it is a natural consequence of intelligence, of paying attention to the world? Knowing this would surely make anguish easier to pursue.

Face it. Things aren't so good. Injustice, racism, sexism, ageism, homophobia, totalitarianism, poverty, war, overpopulation, plastics in the oceans, gullible voters, changing climates, rudderless governments, threats to health care, burgeoning public debt, declining services, water shortages, unaffordable rents, vanishing species, shoddy construction, threatened parkland, police shootings, gun proliferation, religious extremism, gang violence, international bickering, conspiracy theories galore, overprescription, underemployment, and lukewarm coffee.

In a world with all these problems, misery should be easy. No wonder there are so few books on it. There are no books on how to get wrinkles either. It's automatic. It's happiness that is difficult.

Let's take that further. Despite your best efforts, you might reflect on the actual circumstances of your life and smile. Reasonable health. Good friends. Warm days. A reliable food supply. The next-door neighbor's new kitten. You need a defense against levity.

Here's one: Happiness is stupid.

In order to be happy, by this reasoning, you have to ignore or be unaware of the larger reality of the world. You have to prance down the street, enjoying the flavor of your lunchtime kebab and ignoring the massive injustices blaring out their presence all around you. Happiness means forgetting the suffering of others, the state of the planet, the corruption in your culture. The only way you can do that is to have no intelligence whatsoever. Smart people are—and should be—miserable.

I once had an extremely intelligent client who had been depressed for many years. As I often do, I asked him to envision himself feeling fine, and then to consider whether there might be any disadvantages to joy. The hidden downsides of getting well often sabotage progress in therapy, so it's useful to bring them into the open.

He said that he had no real hope for our work, because he could see no way of being cheerful while knowing what he knew about the world. The only happy version of himself that he could imagine was one in which his IQ had dropped fifty points.

To him it was not merely understandable that he was miserable—it was necessary. He scorned the cheerful people around him, who seemed to be living in a dream world. Being happy was naive. The only way to achieve it was to drink the Kool-Aid, believe what you're told, and shut your eyes.

Being happy is even, some might say, immoral. It says that the suffering of others is irrelevant. As long as one child is hungry, you should never be happy.

This mental stance is one you can emulate. Misery, rage, and embitterment are signs of intelligence, of being a thoughtful citizen, a good person. Hold them as points of pride and look down on those who do not share them as fully as you do. Stand guard against joy, against love, against contentment, against gratitude, against happiness. Believe that misery is not just understandable, not just honorable, but useful. After all, only those who see the problems can solve them.

But for this to work, you must:

- Ignore the fact that misery is debilitating and tends to make people less effective at solving problems and taking action, not more so.

- Push aside the realization that your own emotional state does nothing, in itself, to change the world's circumstances. No hungry child is nourished by your tears.

- Disregard intelligent or ethical people who do not seem miserable despite having an intimate knowledge of global problems. The Dalai Lama? Melinda Gates? Malala Yousafzai? Close your eyes to those you admire who are not themselves paralyzed by sadness.

- Above all, allow not a moment's awareness of the fact that others—including thoughtful others—do not see world peace, the eradication of disease, and ultimate justice as prerequisites for enjoyment, laughter, or appreciation.

Focus instead on the outrageous unfairness of modern society. Declare it a uniquely corrupt and despicable culture, the times we are living in uniquely stressful. Avoid comparing it directly with other times or cultures, lest you run the risk of discovering that the alternatives are even worse.

If there isn't enough misery on the surface for you, look beneath it. Become an expert on the various conspiracy theories making the rounds. The moon landings never happened, 9/11 was an inside job, and (in an unprecedented show of clandestine international cooperation) aircraft contrails are seeding the atmosphere to combat climate change and control our thoughts. Believe them all.

If none of these inanities suits you, there are variations of each and thousands more besides. Remind yourself of the obvious: governments do have secrets, they do engage in acts of which their electorates would not approve, and they do have more information on you than you likely feel comfortable with. Then run with it.

Don't be happy. It looks foolish.

Depend on Talent

Aristocracy is so tempting.

When it first appeared, *Star Wars* touched people's hearts and minds. Penetrating beneath the despair of conflict, death, and war, the story posited a unifying, egalitarian principle underlying all life, from the most noble humans to the lowliest lichen. This principle, the Force, could be tapped into and employed for good or evil. And it was in everyone.

Within a half hour of the opening credits, however, the epic slid into a treatise on inborn, virtually practice-free talent. Luke, it turns out (and as we have discussed), is not like other people. He's special. "The Force is strong with this one," intones Darth Vader, who should know. Obi-Wan Kenobi introduces the concept to young Luke and, in a single space-jump of unclear duration (though no one seems to have slept), trains him in enough of the basics to get by. It takes longer to become a barista.

How did he manage it? Luke, it turns out, has a capital-T Talent that, for the most part, is inherited. Most humans and aliens are, in effect, Muggles, whereas a chosen few are godlike in their easily tapped powers.

Myth resides beneath the surface of a culture, in the assumptions and outcomes of its stories. Western cultures, while pretending to have thrown off the shackles of class, continue to rely on the idea of a spine of specialness laid down at birth. Its most recurrent theme is the notion of talent.

I'm as vulnerable to a belief in native talent as anyone. In high school I took two years of guitar classes. I was relatively lazy and acutely self-conscious about the noise I was inflicting on others, so I seldom practiced and developed the firm conviction that I had no musical ability whatsoever. I thought the same thing about my capacity to learn French. So why would I bother practicing? Why slam my head against the brick wall of my nature? I never learned the guitar and still can't ask for a restroom in Paris without the waiter switching sadly to English.

How is a belief in talent an asset on the road to misery? Easy. Most people don't have it. In most areas that will include you. Orthopedic surgery? Quantum mechanics? Tuba playing? Screenwriting? Business management? Automotive repair? Swimming? The best guess in every case is that you will lack the magic juice.

It would be foolish to spend years of your life attempting something that will forever elude you. Better to conserve your resources and wait to be conked over the head with a revelation of your true talents. The Obi-Wan of hotel management or double-entry accounting will one day appear, unveil your mystery talent, and in a few minutes unlock your miraculous skill at coordinating conventions or issuing payroll.

Practice, in other words, is a delusion. You've either got a knack for something or you don't. And you probably don't.

Believing in talent will inevitably make you vigilant for signs of its presence in early experiences. You'll strum a guitar and listen for music; attend a Cantonese class and see if you master the tones. The absence of these signs will mean there's no point in trying. You'll give up, or continue only halfheartedly, and the result will confirm your impression. "See? I told you I'd never learn the backstroke." The belief in your lack of talent will become ever stronger as you abandon interest after interest. You will create the reality you fear.

Just be careful not to ask your idols how they developed their skills. This will pop the balloon. The guitar virtuoso will speak of practice, and lessons, and discipline, and having a guitar constantly nearby to be picked up in moments of idleness. The physiotherapist will talk about university, and anatomy classes, and practicum settings, and repetition, repetition, repetition. The writer will talk about writing. Constantly. While I don't know your individual idols, I do know that each of them achieved success not by being tapped by some unshaven hermit in the Tatooine desert but by putting in years of dedicated practice.

How much practice? The much-discussed "10,000-Hour Rule" points out that mastery in almost any field comes from thousands of hours of rehearsal and repetition. The actual number was never intended to be taken seriously—it was simply a way of saying "a whole lot." In some fields it might take 10,000 hours to become a master, and somewhat less to be "good enough."

- A violin virtuoso might need all those hours or more; whereas a bit less might do for a second violinist or a high school band teacher.

- Appendectomies might safely be handed off to young surgical residents, whereas heart-lung transplants might require far more experience.

- It might indeed take ten years in a pool to get on to the Olympic team, but much less to be the local lifeguard.

Is talent irrelevant, then? Of course not. If you are tone-deaf, you are unlikely to sing *Rigoletto* at the Met. If you can't tell up from down, Cathay Pacific doesn't want you flying their Dreamliners. The vast majority of pursuits, though, do not demand that you be the one in a billion gifted with the musical/surgical/athletic/intellectual equivalent of the Force. You can be a physician, a musician, an engineer, an entrepreneur, a skier, a therapist, a gemologist—and dedication and practice will count for much more than inborn talent.

Even some barriers that might seem insurmountable can be overcome.

- Harvey Pekar became a widely respected author of underground comics despite being unable to draw. He wrote the stories and farmed out the drawing to others.

- Morton Doran became a highly successful surgeon even though he had Tourette syndrome and the attendant vocal and gestural tics.

- One of my best friends is an ornithologist/ conservationist whose audiological impairment has failed to stop him: his twin hearing aids can be tuned to magnify the bird calls he searches for in his fieldwork.

Relying on talent is an excellent path to misery. It nurtures our incapacity, undermines our perseverance, encourages our anguish, and blinds us to the truth: practice and sweat are almost always the larger determinants of success.

You Need a Clear Vision

Let's imagine that receiving a salary and lasting long enough to collect a pension isn't your goal. You'd like to accomplish something a bit more grand. Create a billion-dollar business, start a movement, solve a social problem, lead a nation. How do you do it?

Memes abound—most of them telling you to ignore practical concerns, dig within to find your shining goal, fix your eyes on the prize, and charge ahead. These are usually advocated by people who haven't actually done any of these things. For best results in your quest for misery—and by best I mean worst—follow their instructions.

But isn't your vision all-important? Let's take a step back and consider the issue.

Freud (again with the Sigmund!) famously divided personality into three components: id, ego, and superego.[14] The id is the source of drive and energy: a volatile and potentially dangerous fuel source sparking unrestrained lust and rage, but also finding expression in other passions. The superego is the internalized voice of restraint, morality, and conformity. The id shouts "I want," and the superego cautions "But you shouldn't."

The ego, in Freud's model, isn't the preening narcissist we usually think of when we hear the word: the self-promoting braggart demanding constant attention and praise. That's more an example of an under-governed id. Freud casts the ego as more of a traffic cop or an arbitration lawyer, mediating between the competing demands of the id, the superego, and the outside world.

Consider an example. Your id wants to reach over and fondle the rear end of that lovely stranger next to you at the bar. The superego blushes that you would ever think of such a thing, and the external reality is that the pub you're in would erupt in violence if you did.

The ego makes you put your hands in your pockets. It dreams up a fetching comment about the band that might succeed in safely getting the attention of the object of your affection. This gives cautious vent to your lust without overstepping either the superego's exacting standards or the social norms of the surrounding world.

At various moments in history, the balancing act can be thrown off by a societal devaluation or overvaluation of one or more of the players in this negotiation.

- In Victorian England, the superego was ascendant. Table legs were skirted to avert the excitation of lust, and social manners became so arcane as to be suffocating.

- In prewar Germany, aggressive impulses were stoked to fire the population into an acceptance of war.

- In 1950s America, a generation shocked by war and fearful of Communism retreated into rigid, stifling conformity.

- The 1960s brought about an id-like rebellion among a generation who saw little justification for the constraints of their elders.

Depending on when and where you live, you might be encouraged to "Go with it; cut loose!" During other times the message might be "Be careful; trouble is all around for those who stray from the path." And sometimes it's more "Just try to get along and don't stick your neck out."

Lately there's been a lot of emphasis on id and impulse, and, more important, a de-emphasis on the constraints of reality. Do what you love, the money will follow. Chase your vision. Dream big! Your task, according to these ideas, is to fantasize about what you want and then pursue it—without checking to see whether it's available or realistic.

Believers in the so-called "law of attraction" go so far as to imagine that the nature of reality itself will simply rearrange to fulfill their desires. By wishing for a specific outcome, you will create a universe in which you are chased by the beautiful, job offers come your way in the coffee shop, and lotteries are yours for the winning.

This is a lovely, seductive idea. It's a shame that the world is stuffed with people for whom wishing did not make it so, and in which the pursued vision turned out to be just that: A vision. A phantom. Not a reality. You probably know some of these people.

A young man once announced to me at a party that his ambition was to make a living creating CDs for local bands. I asked him when he had last purchased recorded music. "I pirate," he said. Hadn't paid for music in years. I suggested that he wasn't alone—most people had consigned their CD collection to the storage locker if they'd ever had one, and few actually paid for the music they download. Sound engineering is a thriving field, to be sure, but CD production? The record labels are struggling to survive, and new companies are at a disadvantage.

Doesn't mean it couldn't happen. Stumble across a new business model and you could be the next Quincy Jones or Jay-Z. But try to follow an existing and stumbling model that hasn't been working this century, and you're setting a course for disappointment. My young friend might as well have chosen typewriter repair, Fortran programming, or elevator operator as his ambition. There are probably successful people in all of these areas—but they survive through innovation and the discovery of narrow niches, not by marching into a field long since abandoned by history.

To be miserable, indulge your id and ignore the world around you. Assume that it will all work out in the end. What counts is your vision, not what the world desires or the market will pay for.

Misery Is Motivating

"The annual report's due next week; I've gotta light a fire under my butt and get at it!"

Metaphors have their limits, and the problem with this one is obvious. If there truly were flames licking your buttocks, you would be unlikely to a) study for the calculus exam, b) practice the trombone, or c) revise your long-neglected résumé. You'd yell, step away from the blaze, butter your booty, and call 911.

The fiery image has been adapted any number of ways, but the core idea references behavioral theory. A negative reinforcer is an unpleasant state (like anxiety, guilt, or burning flesh) that ends when we do something desirable like, say, vacuuming the dog hair out of the carpet. The feeling of relief gets associated with vacuuming and makes us want to do it more often. In other words, misery produces results. To achieve something, impose a state of misery on yourself. You'll do whatever it takes to escape it.

Experience suggests to many of us that this actually works. Before tackling unpleasant tasks, we feel a sense of pressure and angst that usually goes away if we get the job done. The leaking sink stops freaking us out when we get it fixed, so maybe it was the freak-out that made us call the plumber. *Post hoc ergo propter hoc*: X happened before Y, so X must have caused Y.

This is a common logical fallacy. One thing happening before the other doesn't make them causally linked. You ate french fries before winning the lottery, but the fries didn't make the right numbers come up. Mother Theresa got famous before Donald Trump, but she didn't give birth to him.

Common experience suggests that misery may help us work harder when we are young. High school students often terrorize themselves with visions of failure as a way to get themselves started on their Pre-Cartesian Models of Literary Criticism term paper. "I'll fail, I'll never get into college, I'll be laughed out of ninth-grade English, I'll wind up living in a tent under a bridge." But around age twenty, this well-learned technique seems to become paralyzing, rather than motivating, for most of us. Still, we hang on to it like a cement lifejacket.

A medical department at a local hospital contacted me for help because an unusual number of their residents were failing their final oral examinations—apparently due to anxiety rather than incompetence. I met with a series of them. It became apparent that they viewed the exam as a pivotal experience in their lives: Pass and they would enter the petal-strewn fields of medical paradise. Fail and they might just as well be taken to the parking lot and shot. (In fact, they'd have to wait a year and take the exam again.)

I suggested that the best way for them to overcome their crippling fears would be to make friends with the possibility of failure. What would they do? How might they go on to have a pleasant life? By de-catastrophizing failure, they could relax a little and their stress would stop interfering with their performance.

Eye rolls of impatience ensued. It was *essential* that they pass. Was I too stupid to see that? Having pushed themselves for years with fantasies of humiliation and homelessness, they believed that their anxiety motivated them to work hard, study, and achieve.

It was only when I led them gently through a recounting of their own experiences that they saw their anxiety not as a motivating asset but as a distracting hindrance. Without it (or with less of it) they would not only feel better but achieve more. They kicked, they screamed, but as their anxiety faded their performance improved, and every resident I worked with passed the exam.

The other day a rather driven friend of mine complained of feeling perpetually stressed about his work managing a restaurant. I suggested he try breathing and focusing on what he was doing in the moment. If he was making a phone call, then just make the phone call. If he was ordering martini glasses, then concentrate on filling in the form. "Look up now and then to see what needs to be on the list, then ignore the list and focus just on the one thing you're actually doing."

"Then nothing will get done," he said. He felt a compulsion to lump all the tasks together into an overwhelming mass. I suggested that he was mistaking the feeling of anxiety for productivity. In fact, the more anxious he got, the more he tended to dart from half-finished task to half-finished task, and far less actually got done. Beyond a certain fairly minimal level, anxiety only interferes with action. It does not fire us up, and it does not help us accomplish what we want to achieve.

For this reason, a firm belief in the utility of anxiety, shame, and self-loathing is a wonderful tool for bungee-jumping into a vat of negativity. It is easiest to accomplish this if you do what my friend did: create a kind of fusion between the emotional state and the results you envision. Your anxiety and your productivity are two essential sides of the same coin. Weld them together until the seam vanishes. Then you will have to choose between two unattractive possibilities: feeling relaxed and sowing the seeds of failure in your life, or feeling tense and failing anyway.

So strike a match and set your bottom alight. Fan the flames. Tell yourself that misery will get you moving. Then settle in and sniff the barbecue.

Mmm. Smells like chicken.

LESSON 17

Self-Confidence Is Crucial

"I would have gone for the swimming lesson, but I didn't feel confident enough."

Sound familiar? Swap out swimming for traveling, interviewing for a job, dating, having sex, joining a club, applying for university, overcoming a fear, eating out alone, moving to a new city, starting a relationship, ending a relationship, having children, hosting a dinner party, taking up skateboarding, acting in community theater, owning a pet, learning to drive, starting a business—anything at all. They all fit.

Sometimes our beliefs are right up front, completely accessible through awareness: "Tossing plastic in the ocean is a bad idea." Many beliefs, though, play out in our speech or behavior whether we are aware of them or not. This one, put more precisely, is "Confidence is a prerequisite for action." In order to try something new, you have to know you can do it.

The moment you put this principle into words, though, the flaw becomes obvious. Why would you feel confident about your ability to swim before you'd ever been in a pool? Believing that you can do something you've never tried is nothing short of delusional. You'll only feel confident once you've done it a few times.

The result of holding this belief is that you have to wait around for your confidence to arrive before you can get started. You'll spend your entire life at home, peering out the front window waiting for FedEx to show up and hand it over. *Et voilà!* Misery.

Most people who are having problems kick-starting their adulthood have restricted lives. They don't go out much, don't take social risks, don't signal romantic interest, don't build their careers, and avoid the unfamiliar. A belief in the importance of confidence is sometimes the culprit. It puts a parking brake on life.

When I suspect this is happening to someone in therapy I try to address it directly. I draw three concentric rectangles on my whiteboard, one inside the other like nesting dolls.

- The zone of comfort is the smallest, and includes situations with which we are very familiar and that we know how to handle. We feel at ease within it, but the longer we stay there the more it shrinks. Items on the fringe fall away and begin feeling uncomfortable. "I feel okay in my own home. Um, except maybe the basement. And the front yard. Oh, and maybe parts of the backyard as well..." Result: eventual misery.

- The zone of extreme discomfort, the largest box, encloses situations that exceed our ability to cope.

These cause an irresistible impulse to flee for safety. If we give in, we experience a surge of relief—and reinforce both the temptation to avoid and the fear we experience when we can't. "No way am I ever doing that again!" Result: more misery.

- The middle box, the zone of mild discomfort, also produces a lack of confidence and the impulse to run, but these can be resisted for a time. "I'm uncomfortable here, but I can stand it." With continued exposure to these situations, the anxiety and the desire to escape tend to fade. Result: initial discomfort, followed by increased freedom—and reduced misery.

You can slot many of your goals or fears into these three boxes. Consider public speaking. Describing a movie to your best friend may fit nicely into your zone of comfort. Explaining a change in the computer system to three coworkers is in your zone of mild discomfort: you sweat a bit but you can do it. Giving a speech at a formal wedding plunks you into the zone of extreme discomfort: you'd rather feign death than attend.

Increasing your misery is easy. Avoid anything that causes the slightest heart flutter and you'll have a smaller and smaller life. Alternatively, you could rush blindly into the wedding speech without any preparation, wet yourself, vomit on the bride, and spend the rest of your life trying to recover from the humiliation.

If you were trying to reduce your misery, you'd put the speech on hold for a bit and carry out multiple forays into the zone of mild discomfort: giving status updates to your work team, asking questions in meetings, proposing toasts at casual dinners, introducing speakers at company events, and leading the warm-up exercise for your dragon boat team. All of these would push your boundaries and stress you out a little the first few times, but your trepidation at giving the wedding speech would diminish as your confidence in public speaking grew.

The more we visit the zone of mild discomfort (taking an indoor climbing course, speaking up in night school, asking people out), the more comfortable we feel. The borders of the zone of comfort expand to include the newly conquered territory. "Climbing five feet used to freak me out; now it's no problem." "Eating alone in a burger joint used to make my hands shake; now it's no problem." "Just getting introduced to someone used to be a struggle; now it's easy." Our confidence shows up late, like a life jacket that turns up when we swim back to the dock.

In the process, tasks that were formerly in the zone of extreme discomfort become imaginable, transitioning to the zone of mild discomfort even though we haven't tried them yet. Having faced the discomfort evoked by the shallow end of the pool, we can inch toward the depths.

For misery, then, set up camp in your zone of comfort. Retain confidence as the gatekeeper to the new.

- You'll never entirely believe you can handle job interviews until you've done some, so you'll be unemployed forever.

- You won't know you can survive romantic rejection until it's happened, so you'll never get close to anyone.

- You can't be entirely sure you're able to live on your own until you've tried it, so you'll have to live with your parents indefinitely.

- You won't be convinced that you can travel alone until the return flight, so you'll be a homebody in perpetuity.

You will spend your entire life trapped within the zone of comfort, eyeing the walls as they inch inexorably inward. The barricades will feel like safeguards keeping danger out, but their actual function will be to keep you locked within.

The zone of comfort is not a nest. It's a jail cell.

For a bigger life, you would need to embrace the reality: confidence is the *result* of taking action, not a prerequisite for it. That ungrounded feeling of tension, that ambiguous fluttering of the stomach, that tremor in the fingertips? They are the normal accompaniment to growth. They tell you that you have cast off the lines and are sailing out into a broader sea. They do not indicate that something is wrong. They are the sensation of your life getting bigger.

For happiness, this feeling of uncertainty is a goal to be pursued. For misery, it is a threat to be avoided.

You're Entitled to Your Anger

When my mother was in the early stages of dementia, it went unnoticed. At one appointment her general practitioner smiled and waved her concerns away. "So you have a few little memory lapses—at your age, you're entitled!"

That wording struck me: *entitled*. As though memory loss were a great reward to be savored, like two scoops of gelato after swimming the English Channel.

The same word gets used with anger: "I'm entitled to feel this way." An odd way of putting it. You're entitled to your hemorrhoids and pink eye too, if you really want them. Hang on tight to those menstrual cramps, you've earned them!

Most of the uncomfortable emotions (sadness, anxiety, fear, shame) are, by virtue of their aversiveness, tempting to discard. Anger, for some reason, we want to hang on to. When we're angry, we often do what we can to keep the fire burning.

This is a great way of bringing on misery, because it's virtually impossible to be cheerful and resentful at the same time.

Here are just some of the ways you can stoke the flames:

- Remind yourself that the targets of your anger—your boss, your workout buddy, your spouse, the tax office, the guy who just cut you off in traffic—have wronged you. This requires action on your part. You have to make them see their inherent lack of consideration. If you let go of your anger, if you relax, if you do not torture yourself, they will get away with it.

- Equate resentment with action. Feeling angry is your way of making your point—even if the guilty party is dead or thousands of miles away and hasn't a clue you're unhappy. "I'll show you," is the stance you want. "I'll make my life miserable and then you'll be sorry." Somehow you'll create a perceptible disturbance and they'll change their ways.

- Even better, get so enraged that you make the situation worse, which will entitle you to be even more angry. Confront the sinner! Rant, accuse, bring up old business, and spray them with saliva. Their defenses will go up faster than a castle drawbridge, and your words will bounce back in your face.

- Exaggerate the crime to goad them into denial. "You have never picked up that dog's turds in your life!" They'll triumphantly show proof of the one time they did so, handily winning the argument, and you can splutter that they've missed the point. Too late.

- Attack their character, which they cannot change, rather than their behavior, which they can. "I want you to have some respect!" "Be smarter about the bills!" They'll either concentrate on growing more neurons—and fail—or they will rightly ignore you.

- If you can't work up a full explosion, just talk about your feelings instead. Recite your reaction to their misbehavior without ever explaining what set you off. "I am furious, and if you don't know what you did, that just proves how clueless you are, so I'm not going to waste my breath telling you!" Their confusion will be further evidence of their lack of consideration, and you can assure yourself that you're in the right.

Above all, avoid examining the past effectiveness of acting out your anger. Don't inventory the number of times the other person shifted their position and agreed that you were right all along. The rarity of such victories runs the risk of undermining your conviction that you are justified and that emoting is the only honest thing to do.

If ranting does bring about the occasional positive outcome ("Well, she did back down and give me the corner desk"), carefully ignore the other consequences (people began avoiding you, you were passed over for subsequent promotions, no one wanted to sit near you at lunch).

If you become aware of the less pleasant results of acting out your anger, use them as fuel for the fire. "If you're honest, you're ostracized." "You have to be a 'yes man' or you're nothing around here." "It takes strength to tell the truth in this organization." Become a martyr. This can be tricky to do. Once you've nailed one hand to the cross, how do you wield the hammer for the other one? The reward of long-term embitterment, however, is worth it.

Savor your momentary resentments and nurture them upward, using them as the seeds of great forests of displeasure. Interpret the delayed reply, the sideways look, the late arrival, the misplaced report, the unmown grass, the broken vase, the burned popcorn as signs of a deeper malignancy: people's fundamental disregard for you and your rights and feelings.

Then magnify your reaction. It's not about the grass, the vase, the popcorn. It's about the person's essential nature as a human being. It's about the pointless and infuriating reality of life itself. Work yourself into a froth, then confront the culprit with full force. Their eyes will widen with surprise and confusion at the intensity of your feeling. Then you can become angry at their lack of insight and their failure to take you seriously.

Harken back to the 1970s, when it became all the rage (so to speak) to get in touch with your anger. People strangled cushions, they beat tires with baseball bats, they screamed at the confines of the birth canal. We called this process "venting" and, without any evidence, believed that it would bleed off pressure from the boiler of emotion held tightly within.

Wrong metaphor, it turns out. We should have thought about a theater stage, not a steam engine. Subsequent research has suggested that those who make a regular practice of expressing their rage become more angry over time, not less.

It's not venting. It's rehearsal.

To be truly miserable, rehearse your fury often. And when, inevitably, your anger begins to cool, remind yourself why you were angry and just how badly you have been mistreated, and it will flare up again into a brightly burning campfire of unhappiness.

Follow Your Passion!

Here are a few of the memes clogging my media feeds lately:

- *"Don't follow your passion: Embody it!"*

- *"Do it with passion or not at all!"*

- *"Follow your passion, and success will follow you!"*

- *"Do what you love, love what you do!"*

- *"If you can't figure out your purpose, figure out your passion, for your passion will lead you directly to your purpose!"*

Renowned mythologist Joseph Campbell arguably started much of this with his phrase "Follow your bliss." Hybridized with fantasy and a desire to avoid practical considerations, this transformed into society's obsession with discovering and chasing after our passions. Nothing else matters. Groaning at the way his words infected the culture, Campbell subsequently commented that he probably should have said "Follow your blisters."

The emphasis on passion and bliss would be easy to avoid if they were just LinkedIn and Twitter memes, but they've become part of the educational system as well. High schools are rife with the idea of discovering one's grand purpose—the activity that causes us to leap out of bed every morning with unrestrained glee.

Which is all just fine if you've got it. I think one of my buddies burned with the flame of orthodontics from the age of ten. But what if you don't?

Ahh. Well, then we have a new path into misery.

- Most fifteen-year-olds have no idea what their passions are. If passion is a prerequisite to finding a life trajectory, then its lack is paralyzing. You have to sit at home waiting for your passions to descend from the sky and land on your shoulder.

- The passions of a teenager are often poor guides to adult life. By the time you age into the field you yearned for as a youth, you may no longer find it so enticing. Furthermore, fields that provoke teenage passions tend not to have vacancies. Not many people will become rock stars, and there are very few jobs in masturbation.

- The people with the greatest passion for what they do often hold positions that they never knew existed when they were younger. How can you have a passion to become an international student recruiter, or a refugee placement coordinator, or a motor vehicle human factors engineer if you've never heard of those jobs?

Furthermore, the way we speak reveals an assumption: passions are "found" or "discovered." In other words, these passions exist already, like Easter eggs hidden in tall grass, and one day we will stumble across them, fully formed. Ask almost anyone who claims to be passionate about their work, though. Seldom was the passion present from the start.

- The architect liked making ever-more-complex models out of balsa wood, but only became interested in human-scale creations in mid-university.

- The wilderness resort operator grew up camping with her father, never thinking that it would become a career.

- The oncologist started looking into melanoma only as a response to grief when his godfather died of the disease.

We stress the importance of passion, then distract people from the reality: *passions are cultivated, not found.*

Most passions begin with a vague interest. You kinda like softball. Helping Dad with the barbecue is sorta fun. Math puzzles help pass a rainy Saturday. As your skills and knowledge deepen, so does your interest—sometimes. You start describing it as a passion only years later. If you'd waited for your passion to run up and curtsy before you, you'd still be sitting on the front porch. If you'd gone hunting for fully formed bliss, you'd have given up in failure by eleventh grade.

The search for passion is, for most, an Easter egg hunt in an empty field. At the outset of adulthood there are few lasting passions, or few worth pursuing. The path forward is through finding and following tiny seeds of interest, seemingly too insignificant to merit attention. We tell people to crane their heads back, searching for oak trees, when what they need are the acorns on the ground.

All of this makes the single-minded pursuit of fully developed passion a greased slide into misery. Either you will cast about endlessly, unable to find a trace of the beast, or you will seize upon a possibility that will drag you off your life's true course.

This does not mean that following your desire to be the next lead in *Hamilton* or *Hamlet* is a guaranteed path to misery. Someone has to play the morbid Dane, after all, and that could be you. But you'll be more likely to fail if you avoid all practical considerations, including:

- Is this something that I like to study in school, or am I truly interested in the career for which it prepares me?

- If Plan A doesn't work out, do I have a Plan B, C, D, and E?

- Am I prepared to accept the possible financial and lifestyle consequences of a career in this field?

- If competition is fierce, are my passion and dedication sufficient to work much harder than I might have to in another area?

- Can I pursue this as an avocation (a side interest that need not support me financially) while cultivating another line of work that will sustain me (even if only temporarily, while I get started)?

The passion chase, especially when divorced from pragmatics, can be as well-trod a path to misery as the rat race. For misery, ignore all considerations of reality. Search for fully formed, irresistible oak-tree passions. If, improbably, you manage to find something that looks like a passion, drop everything and pursue it without considering any alternatives. The best way to run off a cliff is blindfolded.

You're Doomed No Matter What You Do

Our last lie in this section isn't as sunny as some of the others, being apocalyptic in nature, and it's one that neither your family nor the educational system likely taught you. It's common, nevertheless, in the culture and social media, and it's remarkably effective at killing the motivation of people who believe in it. It's this:

It's pointless to go to all the effort of creating an adulthood that will not exist.

The course of your life and death is laid out by forces that are simply out of your control. You're like an ant trying to move a pebble in the face of an oncoming flood. Your efforts are irrelevant, so it's best to conserve your energy and amuse or distract yourself in the short time left before the world ends.

There's no shortage of voices promoting this point of view. Global warming, nuclear proliferation, Ebola, economic collapse—there are various scripts for catastrophe. Some (alien invasion, zombie apocalypse) seem remote, while others are genuine (the climate really is changing and really will produce global effects).

The human brain is designed in large part to help us detect and evade danger. In an environment with hundreds of signals that we are safe and one signal that danger lurks nearby, we have a bias to pay attention to that lone alarm bell.

Great—that's probably why our species is still around. This inclination influences the messages we are attracted to, however. The "good news" websites that crop up every few years invariably go bankrupt. It's the promotion of fear that gets the views and the ad dollars. Your favorite news site probably has a few cheerful stories, but it's dominated by a) the bad things that have happened, and even more by b) bad stuff that hasn't happened yet but could occur in the near future. The preponderance of disaster in the news may have more to do with human neurological wiring than with a balanced portrayal of external reality.

Catastrophe is also an easy and entertaining substitute for good writing. The 1970s were the era of the star-filled disaster movie: earthquakes, fires, air crashes, belly-up cruise ships, and shark infestations. Today's action movies specialize in end-of-the-world scenarios: climate collapse, nuclear winter, pandemics, asteroid strikes, and ape takeovers. Look at the sci-fi and action categories of your favorite movie-streaming service. Count the number in which either the fate of the entire world is in danger or the worst has already happened and a scattered band of brave survivors attempt to pick up the pieces while getting bumped off one by one.

Couldn't one or another of these disasters happen? Probably not the sharknados or the various permutations of Godzilla, but some are surely valid. There really is a big volcano under Yellowstone Park, and SARS almost did escape into the broader population in 2002–3. This can make the worry seem unique to our times, but it isn't. Every decade has had multiple signals of the apocalypse that might have seemed, at the time, to be a good reason to give up on existence and hide under the covers. Consider a few examples:

- 1900s. Strife from industrialization and massive social change. The Tunguska event, US presidential assassination, and an increasingly tense situation in Europe.

- 1910s. The Russian Revolution. World War I and the 1918 Spanish flu, which killed far more people than the war.

- 1920s. The rise of totalitarianism in Russia and across Europe. The Red Scare in the US.

- 1930s. Economic collapse, the Great Depression, mass unemployment, the Spanish Civil War, and the rise of Nazi Germany.

- 1940s. World War II. The Holocaust. The Red Scare (again), and the decline of the US into McCarthyism.

- 1950s. The rise of the nuclear threat and the Cold War. The failure of Western power to win the Korean War.

- 1960s. The Cold War continues, the Vietnam War drags on, and race riots and social strife appear in the US and elsewhere. Multiple assassinations. China's Cultural Revolution.

- 1970s. Multiple terrorist groups cause attacks across Europe. Watergate and disillusionment with American leadership. The rise of disco.

- 1980s. Increasing tensions between the US and USSR. Predictions of nuclear war. HIV/AIDS kills half a million Americans and tens of millions worldwide.

- 1990s. Y2K is predicted to bring computing and the Internet to a halt. AIDS continues unchecked.

- 2000s. 9/11. Wars in Afghanistan and Iraq, amid fears of continued terrorism. The financial system comes close to falling apart in 2007–8. Climate change, first predicted in the 1800s, accelerates and enters the public consciousness.

Despair is the conviction (not just the suspicion) that there is no hope of escape from feared futures. It is just as much a temptation as fear or rage, and it is more effective than either at producing distraction and inaction, thereby perpetuating itself. It is the very essence of a miserable life.

To bring it on, dwell on the fears of the moment. Scan the news for disaster and the intimations of doom. This is easy; they'll usually be on the front or home page. Tell yourself that you are living at a unique moment in history, and that this time, for certain, there is no hope. Ignore the fact that those in every previous decade could also find justifications for such a conviction.

The payoff is not just in unhappiness but also in leisure time. You don't have to work for a future that does not exist. No need to study, build your skills, save for retirement, plan a career, quit smoking, go to the gym, or make the bed. You can finally ignore all the advice that everyone has been giving you and relax. Retreat into a video game or binge-watch television.

It may not be fun. But it will be easy.

PART THREE

Creating a Self

A big part of growing up is bringing all of yourself into a space, not just the parts of yourself that relate to the people in the room.

—*Lin-Manuel Miranda*

Let's say, for the sake of argument, that you are so thrilled with this book that you want another copy to give away. Given the title, that's probably a passive-aggressive thing to do, but fine. Head to a bookstore (if you can find such a thing) and look around. Where's it going to be? Self-help. Books to help you with the self. There aren't any shelves for the production of misery, and they have to put it somewhere.

This begs the question, "What, exactly, is a self?"

Check the media: they're full of the self. *Take care of your self. Be your self. Love your self. Value your self.* And, perhaps more than any other: *Express your self.* Take something from the inside, and squeeze it out into the world.

In his book *How to Have a Lifestyle,* bon vivant Quentin Crisp criticizes the emphasis our society places on self-expression, seeing this as an essentially excretory view of human personality. At birth we don't have much to express other than urine and poop. We may have some nascent personality characteristics (such as shyness/extroversion or cheerfulness/irritability) but these exist mainly as potentials, not as fully formed aspects of a coherent identity. We are not-quite-but-nearly blank slates. No language, few opinions, little experience, a couple of basic tricks, and virtually no entertaining stories to tell at dinner.

The self of a newborn, in other words, is mostly a foundation for what might be built atop it. An excavation. In order to have a self to express—and one that others may someday want to know—we have to install floors, raise walls, fit windows, and tilt up staircases. The self is mostly an act of construction installed atop whatever characteristics and inclinations we bring with us from the womb.

Misery is easy: no hard hats or dump trucks required. Just move in to the raw, uncovered basement and declare it finished. Complain when no one wants to hunker down there with you. Cry out that people aren't looking at your potential.

The alternative is to jettison the idea of the self as a product fully formed at birth—something we inherit or awaken within. Instead, we can view it as a framed canvas that we fill in with our lives. Crisp suggests that whatever else you may be, you are an artist first. Your single most important artwork is your self. Pick up a brush and choose. The *Mona Lisa*? David Hockney's swimmer? Munch's *Scream*? A collie playing poker? Or a blank canvas untouched by the paint of life?

Consider your own ideas about your future.

- You imagine you'd like to be a translator for the United Nations. Fine, but at birth you had no understanding of any language whatsoever. You picked up one tongue at home, and likely studied it at school to the point that you could sass the teacher. To be a translator, you will need to learn at least one more.

- You envision yourself as a photographer. Great. But at birth you didn't know a photograph from a pointillist painting, let alone how to maximize your depth of field. Lessons and practice are required.

- You want to be physically strong. Lovely, but the only exercise you got in the womb was kicking against Mom's abdominals. This bruised *her* six-pack; it didn't do anything for yours.

- You want to be a wonderful and valued sexual partner. Terrific. But good sex is a set of learnable skills, not an instinct. Plus, if you are heterosexual, you have zero experience of the opposite gender's body from within, so you're going to have to discover everything that feels nice and every tweak and nibble to avoid.

- More than anything, you want to be known as a loyal friend. Not bad. It is your relationships that will contribute more to your life satisfaction than anything else. But this involves a huge number of social skills which, like every other kind of skill, need to be mastered and rehearsed.

Aiming for misery instead? Simple. Rely on your DNA. Focus on the expression of the self to the exclusion of its construction. Long to extrude what you have, though most of it is common to us all: emotion, sensation, impression, impulse, poop. Lament that no one seems to listen for very long, that the marketplace for raw humanity is so flooded with unwanted product. They are unjust! They don't appreciate you!

To shape yourself to your ambition you would have to learn a great deal that you did not come into the world knowing. Whatever you might wish to be—a lifelong traveler, a medievalist, a wonderful mother, a yogi, a hunter, a ski bum, a Nobel prizewinner in chemistry—the apps installed at the factory are not sufficient. If your aspiration is to be a deep-sea diver, you'll need to learn a great deal about underwater survival that could never be gleaned from floating naked in amniotic fluid.

To reach fulfillment, fill the watering can, the blender, the paint palette with the elements you'll need in order to create the self that you want to express, and that the world may want to hear from. Have experiences. Learn skills. Practice habits. Construct the person you want to be and gather the resources you'll need.

Even on this personal-development path, misery lurks as an option. Do it entirely for the world around you: parents, friends, smitten hangers-on. They'll want you to be something to which you don't aspire: cisgender, devoutly religious, accomplished with accounting, sexually compliant, agreeable to every expressed idea, silent when attacked, willing to work for a pittance. They may hold out the promise of cash, love, or fame if you go along, paving the road to tears with fool's gold.

Happiness or misery? The self you create will determine the direction you take. Whatever you wish it to be, don't imagine it was there when you took your first post-vaginal breath. It wasn't.

In this chapter, then, let's review a set of strategies either to avoid self-creation altogether or to produce a version that elicits aversion.

Keep Your Tool Kit Empty

How do you start up a restaurant, a carpentry studio, or a ski hill? You need the space and the furnishings—the oven, the lathe, the chairlift. To get all these you need money. Capital. Without the capital, you have no product to offer.

Now—you want to be a sound editor, a sommelier, a rapper, a motorcyclist, a backyard gardener. What do you need? The skills. Meg Jay, author of *The Defining Decade*, calls these, collectively, your identity capital.

The day you emerged into the world, skill acquisition became one of the central missions of life. You learned to talk, walk, cross the street, tie your shoes, eat with a fork, make your bed, dress yourself, ride a bike, count to ten, say the alphabet, read, do arithmetic, catch a ball, fasten your seatbelt, play with friends, sit still, work the remote, rake leaves, climb a tree, spit without hitting your shoes, write a sentence, draw a picture, knot a rope, leash a dog, and hide when the lawn needs mowing.

In business, the phrase "stick to your knitting" means focusing on what your company is already best at. If you're a plywood manufacturer, don't diversify into the space industry. If you're a cake decorator, don't offer pedicures.

In human terms, the phrase suggests trying to get by on your existing skill set—or the basics you learned in school. This is a reliable path to unhappiness. The aforementioned Meg Jay points out that one of the primary ways people get mired in misery-inducing paralysis is to spend their twenties engaged in pastimes that do nothing to increase their competency or that make them experts in something that two years from now no one will care about (I'm looking at you, Grand Theft Auto).

Neglecting to diversify our skills leaves us unequipped in two ways:

1. We are powerless to cope with many of the challenges that life will toss our way, with or without our bidding (falling off a boat, having a family member suffer cardiac arrest, coping with a flat tire on a deserted road).

2. We are unable to live the life we envision for ourselves (capable of whipping up a killer tapenade, ice skating without breaking limbs, or performing an appendectomy).

For a more fulfilling life, you would have to look at not only the skills that might be handy now but also the ones that your intended future self (the diplomat/snowboarder or firefighter/wrestler) would need in order to succeed. Some of these you already know about and could list in twenty minutes; others you'd only discover by talking with people already living out your dream life.

I asked friends and colleagues about the non-work-related skills that have proven valuable in their own lives. The range is truly enormous, too much so to reproduce in its entirety here. Learn just some of these and your capacity for unhappiness might be inadvertently impaired. If, however, you avoid the ones relevant to your own life, endless frustration is assured. Think of it, then, as your "To Don't" list:

- Sew on a button, hem pants, unclog a toilet, perform basic plumbing, assemble Ikea furniture, change a tire, swap out an exhaust system, paint without mess, replace an electrical switch, remove Bolognese stains from a shirt, and install tile.

- Swim, catch a ball, sink a basket, kayak, ice skate, ride a bicycle, bowl, hit a tennis ball, scuba dive, coach kids' sports, avoid avalanches, build a proper fire, read a map, use a compass, and survive in the wilderness.

- Write a budget, manage investments, stay out of debt, perform double-entry accounting, write a will, dye hair, shave without blood loss, dress for a formal wedding, speak a foreign language, pack a suitcase, negotiate the Paris Metro, test blood glucose levels, and vote.

- Meditate, conduct a funeral, teach yoga, recite a sonnet, do stand-up, write a novel, fly a helicopter, offer a toast, breathe with the diaphragm, give a massage, drive, and perform card tricks.

- Debone a chicken, make soup stock, whip up pizza from scratch, shuck an oyster, make an omelet, select an artichoke, create homemade liqueurs, carve a turkey, make poutine, source food locally, cook Italian, use chopsticks, and host a dinner.

- Set workable personal goals, be patient with others, understand child psychology, resolve conflict, manage projects, share feedback effectively, communicate without a shared language, say no, ask for a date, make conversation, and introduce oneself at a party.

- Type, operate a computer, design a website, navigate Tinder/Grinder, spell, construct a sentence, write a résumé, conduct a job interview, speak loudly enough to be heard in a large hall, draft a press release, and talk so a politician will listen.

- Spin wool, knit, play the violin, tune a guitar, sketch, prune a fruit tree, grow tomatoes, repair an irrigation system, relocate a rattlesnake, train a dog, frame a photograph, and give injections to a sick cat.

Most of these aren't essential to existence. Live long enough and you will be astonished at the knowledge some folks manage to do without. A physician friend of mine had no idea there were circuit breakers in his home. A corporate lawyer needed a seminar from his partner to turn on the vacuum cleaner. A houseguest proved completely unfamiliar with the process of making a bed.

The only way to *be* something (an artist, a meditator, a rabbi, a builder) is to *do* something. It is most often through our behavior that we define our nature, and it is solely through our behavior that others know us. For almost everything we might hope to become, there is a requisite set of skills that enable the doing. Those aiming for happiness spend their twenties (and beyond) filling the toolbox.

For misery, leave it empty. Stick to what you already know. It's easier.

Define Thyself

A man with a fauxhawk put up his hand after a talk at the local meditation center.

"You said that the ego is something to overcome, but isn't the whole point of life—early life, anyway—to find out who you are, and strengthen your ego and sense of self?"

The speaker, wearing the maroon robes of a monk, sat uncomfortably for a moment, seeming to radiate regret at having to teach Buddhism to affluent suburbanites. English mixes up so much that Tibetan parses—ego, self, knowledge. There's never a translated word that maps exactly onto another without any corners dangling off the edges.

The monk chose the diplomatic route.

"Well, both: know and not know. Understand a part of yourself so that you can let go and not fear not-knowing. Or know that you change."

It was question period, after all. Almost time for everyone to go home. The fauxhawk had inadvertently opened a can of worms that could take until dawn to sort out.

Western culture and psychology have emphasized the idea of the self as a kind of religious dogma. We mark out the boundaries of our nature like a dog peeing in all corners of its yard. I am compassionate, I am a spiritual person, I am uncoordinated, I am a Myers-Briggs INFP, I am a creative, I am a seeker, I am an entrepreneur, I am a Scorpio, I am a macchiato-drinker.

All of these things are generalizations, categories, labels—and lies—that anyone seeking misery would do well to embrace. Where is your macchiato right now? The term defines you only at the counter of your local coffee shop, and last year it was chai. Are you a cyclist right now, while you sit behind the wheel of your SUV?

We often define ourselves based on thoughts, feelings, or actions that are present a vanishingly small proportion of the day. Every definition takes the full range of human experience and possibility and cuts it back to create a tightly confined silhouette of a human being—when a degree of ambiguity might be more comfortable. I may see myself as a traveler, but how does that describe me when I'm at home? Aussie comic Hannah Gadsby points out that, based on time spent, she is far more of a tea-drinker than a lesbian.

- If you're a creative, how do you make sense of the brainstorming meeting when you can't come up with a single idea?

- If you're an introvert, where does the party planner with the five-thousand-song track list come from?

- If you're a straight dude, why are you looking at that ripped guy at the gym?

We could go so far as to say that the more you think you know yourself, the less you really know. Your "knowledge" consists of beliefs about what you're good at (ignoring the fact that you're sometimes not so great at those things), what you like (even though you don't want it right now), what you're lousy at (which you could get better at it if you tried), and what you dislike (mostly but not always). It accentuates the common (80 percent of the time if people offer me steak I'll eat it) but snips away the rare (occasionally I'll eat oysters and not gag). You think you're no good at sports, but you learned to paddle a canoe at age seven. Firm up the boundaries of your self-definition and you will avoid physical activity forever. Canoeing will vanish, oysters will repel, muscles won't appeal, and all of the associated satisfaction will be safely excised from your life.

Every label is like a lobster's carapace—an enticingly cozy shell that quickly proves too small and begs to be shed. Much of our self-knowledge isn't knowledge at all—it is an edited version of reality, a comforting security lock on the door to a larger life.

So go for it. If misery is your goal, cut yourself off from the 10 percent, the 20 percent, the inconsistent, the surprising. You're shy, remember, so don't go to that after-hours club. You hate spicy food, so don't visit India. You're risk-averse, so whitewater rafting is out. You're an artist, and people like you don't do math. You're a traveler, so settling down isn't an option.

Ask a dozen elders to reminisce about the turning points in their lives and their self-understanding. Most of their answers will involve discovering the falsehood of something they thought they knew about themselves.

- "I thought I was weak and then I survived cancer."

- "I assumed I was unlovable until Jamie appeared in my life."

- "I considered myself a homebody until I backpacked through Cambodia."

Or, generically, *"I thought I was X and turned out to be X and sometimes Y."*

When we define ourselves, whether as X or as not-at-all Y, we winnow our options, snip off bits of our personality, and dismiss opportunities that don't match our sharply outlined vision. We build a life based on our theory, rather than on who and how we happen to be in the moment.

The alternative is far too unpredictable.

- "I haven't done that but I'll try it."

- "In this moment I am not feeling introverted."

- "I'm not comfortable, but I can do it."

- "Maybe I'll have the oysters."

This avoidance of pigeonholing yourself would, were you to try it, produce a wavering, indistinct sense of identity. You might start a self-portrait, then have to erase and begin again on a bigger scale. Do this for eighty years and the paper will be ragged from all the rubbing out. You'll know less than when you began. You'll become a twenty-first-century version of the expansively inconsistent poet Walt Whitman:

Do I contradict myself?

Very well then I contradict myself,

(I am large, I contain multitudes.)

Best not. Your skin isn't big enough to stretch over multitudes. Where is your *consistency*? Where is your *identity*? Start your self-portrait and stick to it. Throw away the eraser. Use permanent ink. Frame it early, and remember: You're not Monet painting a lily pond. You don't need a large canvas. Make it a miniature. A cameo. Preferably in simple black and white.

For a clear, reliable, consistent, and miserable existence, define the limits of your self-constructed shell and live within them. It'll be comfortable at first. You'll know who you are.

But wait a while. The pressure will build.

Become Your Diagnosis

On the first day of my undergraduate abnormal psychology course, the professor began with a discussion of the various types of explanation used by clinicians.

- *Causal* explanations look for the origins or development of a phenomenon. How did it come about?

- *Teleological* (or functional) explanations identify the aims and benefits of a phenomenon, with the presumption that these drive its occurrence. What is its purpose?

- *Classification* identifies the links between related phenomena, showing where they are distinct and where they are similar. What is this like, and how is it different?

- *Labeling* supplies a name for the phenomenon. What'll we call it?

Of these, the least useful is labeling. For the most part, psychiatric diagnosis is simply labeling in action. It doesn't tell us what function the symptoms serve, it doesn't say how they came about, and it doesn't situate them relative to other problems. But if you say "Ahh, he has a depressive disorder" it feels like you've accomplished something and deserve to stop off after work for an appletini.

Labeling yourself, it turns out, is also a great way to restrict your life and maximize your misery. Let's consider how.

Human beings thirst for understanding—of the world, of the future, and especially of our own lives. This desire is so strong that once we've got a theory about ourselves we resist relinquishing it, even if it's painful or inaccurate. Try talking a friend out of their conviction that they are stupid, or worthless, or unlovable, or ugly. You'd think they'd be as eager to cast away these ideas as a hot ember down the pants, but no. Not even when they lead to actions that harm their own interests.

- *Because I am unemployable I never apply for jobs.*

- *Because I have social phobia I never practice the art of conversation.*

- *Because I have attention deficit disorder, there's no point in working on my ability to concentrate.*

Worse, if the theory wasn't true when they first adopted it, it can become true over time.

The various diagnoses we are given can seem to explain our behavior. "Why am I so particular about pointless things?"

"Because you are obsessive-compulsive." "Oh. What does that mean?" "It means you are really particular about pointless things." This is just circular reasoning in action. We want to understand ourselves, so we grasp the diagnosis tight. It may never occur to us to say, "Um, how does that tell me something new?"

Once a person has been diagnosed with a mental quirk or disorder, it can become a seemingly fixed part of their identity. The diagnosis gets strapped into the driver's seat.

- "Why aren't you going to the party?" "Well, I'm on the autism spectrum."

- "Want to take a course on geography?" "No, my evaluation anxiety will make me fail."

- "Aren't you hiking today?" "No, I have depression and it's acting up."

Rather than encouraging behavior that may shrink a problem, diagnosis often promotes behavior that worsens or prolongs it. Therein lies its value for the perpetuation of unhappiness.

Furthermore, once diagnosed we can hang on to the label for dear life. We seldom do this with physical diagnoses. "Want to kiss me?" "Nah, I was diagnosed with a cold three years ago." We see most physical diagnoses as temporary, while mental diagnoses get absorbed as permanent aspects of who we are. They brand our souls. Left unquestioned, they can dictate and limit our lives.

Well, fine, but what if the diagnosis is valid?

It may be. But just as physical illnesses often pass, so do mental ones. Our weak lungs might make us vulnerable to pneumonia, but this doesn't mean we have pneumonia all the time—only that we will probably have it more often than cousin Griselda. In the same way, a depressive episode clearly indicates that we are prone to depression, but we'll likely still spend most of our life non-depressed. Seeing ourselves as depressive may bring about a lifestyle that will magnify the depression and restrict our lives in so doing.

Also, many diagnoses are not particularly valid. Clients often arrive at my clinic having been handed a diagnosis by previous care providers on the basis of a five-minute discussion. The disorders they describe might be real, but the severity and duration criteria are often ignored, and their intermittent nature is de-emphasized.

One day, in a moment of frustration, I raised a question on the discussion page of my local psychological association: *Are you finding it easier to diagnose people, or to un-diagnose them when the diagnosis was clearly wrong?* The consensus was that it was easier to provide an explanation than to retract a mistaken one. We hang on to our labels. They become our identification tag, as much a part of us as our name.

If you have been given a diagnosis, it may well be accurate and helpful in your particular case. The problem it describes may be a genuine part of your experience and history. It may even, in some unexpected way, enrich your life.

Your label may also suggest a course of action. Treatment almost always involves pushing one's behavior in the opposite direction of the diagnosis: taking your emotions out of the driver's seat if you tend toward borderline personality disorder, getting out of the house if you are depressed, loosening the rules if you are obsessive, seeking out heights if acrophobic, or speaking up if socially anxious.

The road to misery is to obey the dictates of the disorder instead. Take your diagnosis as a script, make it your identity, and lead your life accordingly. Become the obstacle that once was only a barrier standing in your way. Make it who you are, not what you have—or once had.

Cultivate Your Fragility

Do a quick inventory of your friends. Reduce them to a single scale: adaptability. Some of them you could take to any restaurant, on any road trip, to any social event. Snow camping? No problem. Meet the governor? Great. Try a yak-milk latte? Hand it over.

With others you have to be more careful. For Andre it's a five-star hotel or nothing. Jessica couldn't handle your crazy aunt. William freaks out if he sees a spider. Rae-Lyn goes ballistic at the friendliest advice.

Now consider: who is happiest?

One way to increase your misery is to shrink the range of circumstances in which you are content. It's hard to control every detail of your life, so getting everything right will almost never happen. If someone gets your name wrong, if the couch is out of place, if the ice cream is melting, if the invitation wasn't made at least a week prior, if the acknowledgment for the work project isn't glowing, you will effortlessly slide into resentful unhappiness. To be miserable, become a princess for whom no pea or pebble under the mattress is too small to be noticed.

The traffic light nearest my home is a long one. One day a man stood beside me, impatient and angry, repeatedly (and pointlessly) pressing the signal button. "Damned light," he said in red-faced agitation. "This is the worst part of my day." I said nothing, but wanted to remark, "How lucky you are." All around him people are dealing with illness, bereavement, financial stress, racism, relationship troubles, addicted children, career instability, bullying, and burnout. The worst part of his day? A long stoplight. How wonderful. It's inspiring to see a master of misery at work.

For a miserable life, magnify your sensitivity. Become adept at noticing your dissatisfaction when things are not precisely the way you like them to be.

- This lull in the party is a sign of how nothing in life is ever really rewarding or fun—and never will be.

- Your undercooked entrée is a reminder that no one really cares about quality—certainly not at this restaurant, where they are clearly just in it to extract as much money from you as they can with the smallest possible effort.

- The single "X" and "O" at the bottom of the anniversary card from your partner is an indicator of their fading love for you—probably because they have found someone new.

- Michelangelo's *David*, now that you see it up close, has a grotesquely big head; even supposed master-pieces are disappointments when you get right down to it.

Cultivate not just your sensitivity, but also your vulnerability to distress when things are not quite right. Be a person whom others must tiptoe around in order to avoid giving offense. Mostly they won't do this, so you will constantly be hurt. "They didn't consider my feelings!" you can shout. Resiliency is for people too stupid to realize they are being insulted, or too numbed by their lives to know any better.

The alternative would be to cultivate strength. Not just physical strength, but the psychological strength to tolerate a wide variety of situations and outcomes. Your burger isn't quite hot enough? You'll live. Friends forget your birthday? Whatever. Flight canceled due to an ice storm? You can sleep at the airport. You still have preferences, and the right to speak up in the face of real injustice. But you won't wither and die if things don't go your way.

In an increasingly diverse world, most of us are members of one or more minorities. As a gay psychologist, I regularly give talks on LGBTQ issues to groups of medical professionals. During one of these, a young dentist expressed shocked dismay when I mentioned socially inappropriate terms to eschew in the clinic. (Let's just say my examples rhymed with "bag" and "bike.")

I hadn't issued a trigger warning beforehand to alert those who might be traumatized by hearing such hurtful words so they could cover their ears or flee into the hallway.

I found myself reflecting on the fact that the LGBTQ community has had the strength to withstand decades of legal, cultural, and theological condemnation, to survive threatened and actual violence, and to have pulled together to care for one another in the face of an epidemic that killed two hundred times more American citizens than the 9/11 attacks. We have worked to create immense social change. My inclusion in the dental school curriculum was itself such a change. Inadvertently, however, we have also cultivated in some a deep belief in their own fragility—a belief that might prove self-fulfilling.

To achieve misery, the path is obvious. Believe that the mere utterance of a word, the slightest glance of disapproval, or the faintest hint of challenge or disagreement is enough to rob you of all your power. Become ever more vulnerable to the attacks that you know will one day come. Have complete and unjustified faith in your own weakness. You'll have plenty to work with. Life dishes out defeats like french fries at a burger joint.

On the social justice front, obviously I don't mean that we should ignore bigotry or tolerate discrimination without comment. Instead, I'm referring to the ability to experience an attack and see that no blood has been drawn—and *then* to respond effectively. Micro-inconveniences, micro-disappointments, and micro-aggressions are survivable. I still get asked if I have a wife; a trans friend still has to hear the wrong pronouns; a third-generation Canadian friend of Chinese ancestry still gets asked where he's from. A quick check of the wrist: yes, our hearts keep beating. Tiresome, maybe. But survivable.

We can even endure life's inevitable disasters: dismissals, desertions, deaths. It's natural to think *Maybe I can't [or couldn't] survive this*, because you've never had to before. How would you know?

One of the most surprising realizations in growing older is just how much pain you can handle, just how many losses you can endure. A book, a mentor, a grandparent can tell you this all they want—you'll only know once you've done it.

For now, cultivate your refinement, your sensitivity, your dissatisfaction, and your ability to sustain a wound from the slightest blow.

Narrow Your Experience

The range of our lived experience determines, to a great extent, our adaptability and the width of our horizons. Misery is best served by a uniformity of personal history.

Here's an example. Our ideas about "what women are like" and "what men are like" are powerfully shaped by the first, the most-often-present, and the most-connected-with-us individuals in our lives. Usually this means our parents. Their influence is stronger if there aren't many other representatives of their gender to learn from. An angry father is more likely to embed the "men are hostile" idea in us—and will do so with greater conviction— if he isn't balanced out by calm or supportive uncles, mentors, and friends.

Diversity in numbers helps us create more nuanced and complex ideas: *adult women can be like this, or this, or this, or sometimes this*. The child-raising village is a great idea in part because it gives the offspring a wide range of experience.

What is true for the genders is more broadly true for life.

- If everyone you know is in the military, then the military can seem like the only logical career path.

- If your only exposure is to the arctic, it's hard to imagine life in the tropics.

- If you were raised entirely in an urban environment, living in a small town might not even occur to you.

- If everyone around you is Lutheran, other religious views will probably feel alien or obviously untrue.

The narrowly consistent elements of your life can fade into the background, unnoticed, unquestioned, and assumed. When, later on, you are exposed to alternatives, these can seem nonsensical, counterintuitive, or even immoral.

- North Americans traveling abroad for the first time often refer to driving on the "wrong" side of the road, feel cheated by restaurant portions of adequate size, and view cultural traditions as quaint examples of a failure to grasp Western concepts.

- Straight cis individuals encountering a trans person for the first time can express wonderment at the idea of gender diversity. "What do you mean sex and gender aren't the same thing?"

- Relatively minor differences in governance can spark fear and denunciation of tyranny, anarchy, or "godless socialism." Example: the horror stories told in America about the universal health care systems operated by every other developed nation.

- Perceptions of alternative cultures or ways of living can be unduly influenced by the distortions of media coverage. At a conference recently I listened while a table of delegates voiced deep fear about European travel, ignoring the far higher crime and murder rates right there at home.

The range of life's possibilities depends to a great extent on the options you have seen and experienced personally. One way to limit your development, then, is to restrict the range of settings, people, and lifestyles to which you are exposed. This can feel safe, comfortable, and uncomplicated, because you will be aware of fewer options and decision making will initially seem simpler. But it will cut you off from many alternatives that might inadvertently lead to deeper fulfillment and a greater appreciation for life.

In the classic *Twilight Zone* episode "It's a Good Life," three-year-old Anthony has godlike powers. At birth he mentally separated the village of Peaksville from the rest of the planet. Out at the town limits, the road simply drops off into blankness, isolating the desperate townspeople in their tiny world.

You can create your own Peaksville, your own segregation. Stay within your social group, your social class, your community, your faith, your nation. Never venture outward. Try nothing new, nothing different, nothing that will challenge your perception that all of the elements of your life are as nature intended (valid and correct), rather than the arbitrary result of the small world into which you were born.

The alternative might be uncomfortable. You would get to know people you've never met, eat food you've never tried, hear stories of people coloring outside the lines laid down by your upbringing, negotiate languages and cultures you don't at first understand, and see a thousand roads you have thus far left untraveled. Along some of these may sit elements of a life that would fulfill you, ideas you could take home, experiences that would change the familiar person you have become. Decisions would become more complicated, your world more nuanced, your life more rich—but your outlook and way of thinking less certain.

Better to take a piece of chalk, draw a line across the road out of town, and spend your twenties—and, why not, the rest of your life—behind it, rocking on your porch in Peaksville.

Don't Rehearse

The dream is virtually universal. You've probably had it.

- It's the day of the final exam and you haven't attended a single lecture of the course.

- It's the opening night of the play and you haven't memorized your lines.

- It's your first day on the new job and you haven't worn pants.

Your incompetence and lack of preparation are about to be revealed for all to see.

What's lacking in all of these dreams is some kind of rehearsal. You are unprepared, lacking some essential element that now, to your horror, will be called upon. Waking life provides these experiences too.

- You land in Madrid and remember that you'd intended to brush up on your high school Spanish.

- You join a pickup basketball game and wish you'd spent more time shooting hoops alone.

- You're called on to present at the sales meeting and regret not giving it a few dry runs in front of the mirror.

- A woman at the next table collapses to the floor and your Heimlich lesson from three years ago vanishes from your mind.

And what have we got? Four flavors of misery, the common feature of which is that in every case you've avoided laying a firm foundation through practice. Maybe you've done the task before—this is probably not the first time you've held a basketball—but it's still awkward, still requires thought at each step. You haven't made it a part of yourself. The result is underperformance, humiliation, disappointment, a sense of inadequacy, and guilt. And desperately needing to pee because you don't know how to ask for the bathroom *en Español*.

Practice doesn't just mean learning a skill. It means automatizing it. Flight attendants often groan when trained, yet again, how to evacuate an aircraft. "We know this already," they cry as they troop into the fake fuselage. The point of the exercise isn't to teach them the steps, but to make the procedure so automatic that conscious thought won't be required in the event of an emergency. They need to find themselves opening doors and shouting instructions without pausing to remember the drill.

The amount of time we've spent rehearsing governs how effectively we defibrillate, or what we do when a puck is shot our way, or when our date produces a condom and raises a suggestive eyebrow. Without repetition, the sequence is likely not readily available, especially when the pressure is on.

To be miserable, reassure yourself that you'll figure it out when the time comes. Rehearsal is just too *planned*. Too cold. Too—gosh—too *competent*.

Much of what we do, through repetition and rehearsal, becomes a behavioral chain that no longer requires much concrete thought: having a shower, crossing the street, brushing our teeth, doing the laundry, saying "thank you" to the barista, mowing the lawn, making lasagna, evacuating an Airbus.

These automaticities simplify behavior and decision making, hugely reducing the "cognitive load" of a sequence. Things we have done a thousand times are easier than those we've only managed once. If you can drive a standard, compare your first time changing gears with how you do it now. Let things slide for a bit, though, and that solid behavioral chain starts flaking apart. If you're good at something, let it go. Eventually you'll be back where you started. Everything old will be new—and difficult—again.

Rehearsal is also relevant when we think about broad elements of character, not just simple behaviors. There's a story that regularly makes the rounds on the Internet. It's usually placed in a Native American context, though its origin is actually unclear.

A man tells his grandson that two wolves fight perpetually within each of us. One is filled with anger, hate, jealousy, and selfishness; the other with kindness, bravery, and love. He pauses for a moment, giving the boy a chance to ask the inevitable question.

"Which one wins, Grandpa?"

The grandfather smiles. "The one you feed."

Point taken. Feeding is rehearsal. With enough repetition, almost anything becomes easy.

Try the theory out for yourself. Start doling out steak to the nasty wolf. Indulge the more negative incarnation of your character and *it* will become more natural, more automatic. The other wolf will sit nobly off to the side, getting thinner and weaker from neglect.

- Give in to your every impulse, telling yourself that at any moment you could do the opposite. Take the drink, check Reddit for the tenth time in a day, sit inert before the TV, smoke up at the slightest hint of anxiety. These behaviors will get easier and easier, and the alternative self that maybe at one point you imagined was the "real you" will disintegrate.

- When online, rehearse your one-sided, judgmental, dismissive, eye-rolling, know-it-all self. Tell yourself that it's harmless and that in person you are completely different. Ignore your contribution to the toxic atmosphere—and the inevitable seepage into your real-world style.

- Neglect the people in your life, or pick at them with criticism, or lecture them with unrequested advice. Treat them as inferior, reassuring yourself that you'll respect them if they prove worthy. By then you'll have forgotten how.

Perhaps you secretly long to be kind, openhearted, confident, brave, fair, generous, and forgiving. Maybe you're tempted to hold off on practicing these qualities, though, sensing that they don't flow naturally from your impulses. You'd be faking it. Believe that your actions should reflect who you are inside.

Ignore the fact that what we do *creates* who we are. We are not kind, or considerate, or loving, until these characteristics appear in our behavior. Once in our repertoire, they become gradually easier to produce—and eventually become automatic. We go from novice to master. Our behavior transitions from aspiration to character trait.

For misery, then, wait for the impulse. One day, perhaps, the magic character fairy will tap you on the shoulder and make you considerate, or courageous, or physically active, or good with kids, or responsible, or punctual, or neat, or precise, or a good dresser, or a Spanish speaker, or a swimmer, or assertive, or sober. Then you can put that self into action without feeling awkward or false.

There are no such fairies in my garden. But maybe there are in yours.

Stay in the Closet

"Oh, at last," you're thinking. A strategy you can skip past, because it doesn't apply to you. Rather than the full forty, you'll have to get by on just thirty-nine paths to misery. They'll do.

Well, not so fast. Give me a minute here.

Imagine that one day you go up to your mother and say, "Sit down a moment. I have something serious to tell you. It may be a bit of a shock. I'm Jewish / black / British / left-handed / male."

She stares at you as though you've lost your mind. "Uh, yeah, I know. We're related, remember? Are you feeling all right? Have you hit your head?"

In most respects, you don't have to reveal your identity to your family. They already know.

Unlike most minorities, LGBTQ individuals have the option to disclose or withhold their identity. If we open the closet door, the reaction can be hard to predict. My family was fine with it and, years later, turned out in force for a raucous wedding that sprinted recklessly past all time limits and bar tab projections.

Many families don't cheer such events, however. Coming out to family is like taking the people to whom you're closest, plunking them down on a roulette table, and spinning the wheel. You can mostly guess how it's going to go, but there are always a few surprises. Some people lose everyone.

That sounds like a road to misery, and it can be. But for most people, staying locked in the closet is a surer path. It's also easier. The decision not to decide can become automatic and go on for decades. Another day of hiding yourself is almost always simpler than the day you decide to reveal who you are.

Developmental psychologists often talk about character formation in the context of *separation/individuation*, a term originally used by Hungarian physician Margaret Mahler to mark an infant's awareness of the distinction between itself and its mother. It may seem obvious that if something—a breast, for example—isn't continuously connected to us, then it isn't a part of us. For an infant, however, this is a revelation.

The term's application to later development refers to a process in which the individual recognizes and eventually declares their distinctiveness and differences from their family of origin. You may be an agnostic, for example, not because your parents are but because it makes more sense to you. You put a dash of chili powder in pasta sauce not because Grandma did, but because that's how you like it. You are in accounting school or tap dancing lessons or vegan dog grooming not because Mom or Dad were, but because you choose to be.

In a word, you diverge.

You can hide that fact, or you can spell it out to people who might reject you for it. Individuation usually involves some form of coming out. For those in sexual minorities, coming out can be one of life's most profound acts of separation/individuation. "I am something you never expected, never planned for, and may never have wanted." Having said some version of that, less profound hurdles are often significantly easier. "Listen, I told my deeply conservative family that I'm trans. If I can do that, I can do anything."

Maybe this still doesn't sound like it applies to you. You may be straight as an arrow and/or the pride of your family, but separation/individuation doesn't just skip a generation to your lesbian kid. One way or another, this is a cup everybody gets passed. You can either drink from it or run away.

For misery, flush it. Hide everything.

But, uh, what secrets are we talking about? They don't have to involve your gender identity or choice of bed partners. There are thousands of possibilities.

- Your thoughts and opinions on social issues, politics, and government.

- Your beliefs about faith, religion, and the nature of reality.

- Your views on personal morality or family—sex, birth control, living together, the value of marriage, the desirability of having children.

- Your ideas about what makes up a worthwhile life or career, the balance between financial security and pursuing your interests, between stability and mobility, between climbing the ladder and holding the ladder for others.

- Your likes and dislikes, however nerdy or remote they might seem to others (your coin collection, your obsession with sitcoms from the 2000s, your love of Cantopop, your fear of navel lint).

One way or another, every day you are faced with the nerve-wracking possibility of revealing something about yourself that others might wrinkle their noses at. You could do the striptease and expose who you actually are, or keep yourself zipped. The choice is always there.

It's so much simpler to hide your individuality beneath a Harry-Potter-esque invisibility cloak. All you have to do is keep your mouth shut. Remain anonymous forever. Crouch closeted among the winter boots and discarded mittens, hearing but not participating in the world beyond the door. Tell yourself that they could never accept you, and that you could never withstand their rejection. The longer you live this way, the more automatic it will become, and the deeper will be your conviction that this is your only option.

If you pretend to be what others expect, eventually it won't be an act. If your interests or beliefs never emerge into the light as open elements of your life, maybe they don't really exist at all. How you behave will become who you are. Your uniqueness—your selfhood—will be more of a fantasy than a reality.

Having lived so long in a closet, you will become one: the silent recipient of other people's coats, hats—and baggage. How could that not lead to misery?

Build Your Brand, Not Your Character

All this personal creation stuff must be starting to sound exhausting. No wonder the road to misery is the one most traveled: it's less work.

If, for some reason, you did want to create a more expansive self, though, where would you begin? One strategy is to bridge the gap between two versions of your own self-image.

- Your actual self. This is the person you are at present—your current habits, knowledge, skills, and behavior.

- Your ideal self. This is the person you aspire to be— what Oprah might call your "best self"—potentially including abilities and character traits you wish to have but lack at the moment.

It's fine if these two visions aren't identical. The ideal self points the way toward growth. We'd love to be able to save our children if they get into trouble in the ocean, so perhaps we'll take swimming lessons. We want to run a marathon, so we'll ramp up the fitness routine. We want to be self-sufficient, so we'll live on what we earn rather than going into debt.

Sounds like a lot of effort, right? As usual, misery is considerably simpler. You don't have to be honest, or courageous, or thoughtful, or informed, or much of anything really. It's enough to make other people believe you are already all of these things. If the online profile succeeds in getting you a date, what's the problem? If your shamelessly padded résumé gets you the position, mission accomplished. If your friends perceive you as successful, does it really matter whether the Rolex is fake, the degree is forged, and the condo is borrowed?

You don't have to live your best life. You don't even have to strive for it. All you have to do is convince the world you're already there. Companies often do this. Rather than going to all the effort of becoming environmentally responsible, they can just put out an ad campaign declaring they're Earth-friendly. It's cheaper and easier.

For our purposes, this approach acts like yeast: stand back and watch misery rise out of the pan. Welcome to branding.

Once upon a time, human beings had rights and privileges not given to abstract entities like companies. Then corporations developed a legal status roughly equivalent to personhood. The identity of these new creatures, this imaginary species, is their brand in the marketplace.

Today the roles are reversed. Humans strive to become as real and successful as corporations, so they adopt the strategy of cultivating a personal brand. It's not about character (who you really are). It's about the image that you project. Rather than working at your skills, habits, and attitudes, focus on manipulating the perception that others have of you.

To this end:

- Use your social media accounts as lifestyle advertising. "Jessica: Freshly tanned on the beaches of Hawaii! Comes with a no-additional-charge Lexus!" "New minty-fresh Jason, now with added triceps (product not exactly as shown)!" Your real life will never quite measure up to the carefully selected snippets you reveal, so you will feel inferior to an avatar that has your name but doesn't actually exist.

- Build up the expectations of people who have never met you, so that your eventual unveiling will be a humiliating disappointment. The very best place to do this is on dating sites, ensuring that even success (meeting someone in analog reality) will mean failure (they find out the truth). They'll prefer your pixels to your pecs, your profile to your personality, your stats to your style.

- Out in public, relentlessly toss in tidbits about your accomplishments and wonderful attributes, true or enhanced. Downplay potential weaknesses, especially the ones people will eventually discover no matter how hard you try. Admit no doubts, no fears, no signs of less-than-superhuman reality. Because no one can really relate to a perfect person, they will lose interest in you even if your mask doesn't slip.

The process of self-actualization—of bringing the actual self into line with your ideal—is one of the main routes to deepening happiness and satisfaction. You'll want to avoid that.

Instead, do the opposite. Create a carefully branded "public self" that diverges from the person you really are. You'll know the truth, and as the moat between you and your public image widens you will experience the opposite of self-actualization. What should we call that? Embarrassment? Shame? Or just misery?

Perhaps you have wondered how the rich, the famous, the apparently successful can so often experience depression, inadequacy, or panic, sometimes to the point of suicide. They seem to have everything; how could they possibly not be satisfied with their lives?

There are many answers, and in my consulting room I've heard a lot of them. One of the main ones is the gap between the adulation they receive for their public persona (the rock god, the financial genius, the sports superstar) and their awareness of their all-too-normal humanity. The toe fungus, the undisclosed failures, the childhood traumas, the fears of aging, the relationship letdowns, the waning interest in what once seemed so exciting, the three-in-the-morning sweats, and above all, the performance anxiety brought about by wondering just how long they can keep up the act. And, if they give up the public self, does there remain an actual self at all, or has it dissolved away in the glare of the spotlight?

The nature of the branding path is that it branches again, just up ahead. The branding either fails, producing misery, or it succeeds, producing misery. You get the prize either way. There are so few guarantees in life. Don't pass one up when it presents itself.

LESSON 29

Eat the Marshmallows

One sunny spring day early in my career, I was walking the hospital grounds with an older colleague on one of his cigarette breaks between clients. We were talking about the then-fashionable concept of the inner child, based on the idea that many adult problems arise, at least in part, from trauma and shame in childhood.

"I don't know," he said. "More people seem to need to find their inner adult, not their inner child."

That may sound as though he was belittling his clients. He wasn't. He was one of the most compassionate and effective clinicians I have had the pleasure of working with—and he was making a valid point. Much of self-creation involves the cultivation of our adult ability to override our impulses.

In the late 1960s, psychologist Walter Mischel began his series of famous marshmallow studies.[15] One by one, young children would be seated at a table before a marshmallow on a plate. The experimenter would say, "You can eat that marshmallow if you like. But I'll be back in fifteen minutes and if it's still there, I'll give you another one, and then you'll have two." This, obviously, is a test of the child's ability to delay gratification for the sake of greater rewards in the future.

Follow-ups showed that the outcome of this simple task is a fairly good predictor of academic success much later on—including SAT scores. No surprise there, you might think: surely it's a test of native intelligence, and brighter preschoolers turn into brighter adolescents.

Not so. Nor is it a marker of inborn character. Subsequent studies examined children's use of various strategies to assist them: distraction, self-talk ("No, you don't want to eat that"), focusing on the bigger future reward, and so on. Leaving the marshmallow reflects the children's use of a cornucopia of techniques that prevent self-defeating temptation from finding expression in behavior. These strategies tend to prove relevant later in life.

Well, terrific. This points out an obvious way to maximize your misery: stuff that marshmallow into your face the moment the experimenter turns around.

Hang on, though. You're not in the study. There's no table, no plate, no hidden camera. Maybe you don't even like marshmallows and could happily leave a bowl of them on the table for weeks. Swap them out for something a bit more tempting, however...

- You've got the makings of a salad in the fridge, but there's a bag of chips on the counter calling out to you ever so faintly. Open it up.

- Your statistics final is tomorrow, but the video game controller is an inch from your right hand. A few more minutes couldn't hurt, could it?

- Tomorrow's meeting is at seven a.m., but your buddy at the pub just ordered another round of Guinness. Take a sip.

- The party's jumping and it's cocaine on the plate, not flavorless candy. Whyever not?

- You could be writing that report for work, but hours of Internet porn are just a click away.

- You're saving for your condo down payment, but just look at those sharp clothes in the mall.

- You're looking for a long-term relationship, but the sketchy guy at the club just invited you home for breakfast.

Booze, drugs, food, spending, gambling, binge-watching, questionable sex, you name it: the world knows your every temptation and manufactures products to make eating the marshmallow ever easier.

Let's put our misery mission on hold for a moment. Most of your life goals, if you have been so unwise as to develop some, involve the ability to stay focused and defer gratification. Travel depends on saving sufficient funds to afford the fare. Being a musician depends on tedious amounts of practice. A long relationship depends on tolerating the other person's inevitable quirks and not running off with a neighbor. Child-raising means changing diapers when you'd rather do anything else. Without the ability to stay on task and not indulge every momentary temptation, very few of your goals will ever be met.

Again, this makes misery *so* easy to achieve. Just do what feels right. Want a beer? Call the bartender. Feel like screaming at your boss? Cut loose. Hear the casino calling to you? Spend your rent at the craps table.

In this you are helped by the physical nature of your brain. Impulses are governed in large part by structures in the brain's primitive limbic system. Impulse control is the responsibility of the prefrontal cortex, the deeply ridged center of executive function shelved just above your eyes.

The prefrontal cortex is a late bloomer among the brain's components, coming into its full power only midway through one's twenties. Before then, it struggles to keep a leash on the impulses, straining and sputtering and sometimes giving out altogether. This goes quite a ways toward explaining why violence, dangerous driving, and ill-thought-through sexual behavior is disproportionately represented in under-twenty-fives—particularly males, who suffer from the twin challenges of a weakling prefrontal cortex and a limbic system turbo-charged with testosterone.

Imagine a devil on one shoulder and an angel on the other, each whispering into an ear. The angel is prissy and self-satisfied, a party pooper with a halo. If it wins out, it gets to install a stoplight between impulse and action, between thirst and the ordering of a drink.

On the other shoulder sits the devil—sexier, cooler, and more fun—lusting after total control. If it gets unrestricted access to the steering wheel, you'll give in to every whim, down every drink, eat every chip, buy every toy, spend every dollar. You'll feel a brief burst of enjoyment each time, but you'll paint another thin coat of deep blue misery on your psyche.

It's not a fair fight. The devil starts out with a hefty weight advantage over the anemic angel, who can only bulk up by weightlifting uneaten marshmallows. By indulging your little red friend you can keep the intersection open, an unrestricted superhighway to gluttony with no stoplights, no speed limit, no rules, and no guardrails.

So next time you see a marshmallow on a plate—or a bottle of scotch, or a remote control—pick it up, open wide, and swallow.

Be Cool

A friend of mine in university had a favorite costume that he wore to Halloween parties several years running. It was a skin-tight, flesh-toned bodysuit with bits of hair sewn into all the appropriate places. The tear-away (and, needless to say, oversize) genitals were attached with Velcro for the shock value of sudden removal. At a glance—on a dark doorstep or in a dimly lit room—he could easily be thought to be completely naked. He wasn't, though—he was wearing just as much as the rest of us. His exposure was a sham, a walking joke.

The true self feels vulnerable. If you are criticized for the cut of a borrowed jacket, the color of a rental car, or the pallor of your skin in clown makeup, it doesn't hurt much. The object of scorn is temporary, trivial, not a part of you. But if, deep in your soul, you love your family, or you believe in your faith devoutly, or you are transfixed by opera or anime, and this is harshly mocked? That hurts more. Their lances stab not at the tweed of your jacket, but right at your heart.

It's tempting to avoid the risk. Hide your emotions, or ratchet them back to the point that they can barely be detected. People can't dismiss what they can't see. In this quest I present you with a hardware-store-socket-set of five strategies.

- *Cool.* This is the art of flatlining your emotional reactions. Whatever happens, whatever you are doing, monitor your behavior. Observers shouldn't be able to tell whether you like something or not. Dancing, arguing, attending a funeral, skydiving? Your expression should be the same. Nothing affects you, nothing changes you, nothing penetrates the languid placidity of your face and actions. There's nothing for others to attack because nothing is visible.

- *Boredom.* Support your cool by genuinely feeling nothing. Cultivate the skill of ennui. Dwell on how predictable everything is, how much it resembles everything else, how rarely genuine novelty appears. Air travel, mountain peaks, whitewater rafting, deer grazing by moonlight, the Sydney harbor? Seen it, done it to death. Learn to yawn at wonder, look distracted at love, sigh at the speed of sound, and complain at the tedium of absolutely everything. If you don't feel bored when you begin, you soon will; and everyone else will be bored by you.

- *Irony.* Is it too difficult to be 100 percent cool? Irony layers a secondary emotion atop the first, creating a labyrinth of potential interpretations. The few people you trust may get your real meaning, but others may be comically befuddled, believing that you're wearing that outfit because you like it, voicing that opinion because you hold it, showing that sentiment because you feel it. They may mock you, but only because they are too stupid to see through your smokescreen while you stand behind it and laugh. It's a defense against being seen, sure, but you can pretend it's sophistication.

- *Cynicism.* The world constantly throws out hooks that threaten to catch your enthusiasm, sparks that may ignite your interest. Avoid capture by cultivating a skeptical attitude toward anything that might look superficially appealing. That candidate may have a nice smile but he's surely corrupt; that charity may seem to be getting results but it's just there to make the founders feel good; that research may be curing lupus but someone has to be making a profit. Take off your rose-colored glasses and put on lenses of the deepest gray. Dismiss the world as impossibly tainted and try to rise above it, weightless and irrelevant. Refuse to "play the game" and infer the worst possible motives in everyone around you. Occasionally you may even be right—but you'll *always* be unhappy.

- *Philosophy.* If enthusiasm still threatens to entice you, retreat into the inner chambers of intellect. A fascinating and worthwhile pursuit of its own, philosophy can also serve as a great avoidance strategy. Question the meaning of everything. Doubt whether you are really here at all. Maybe what seems to be reality is actually like something out of *The Matrix*: a dream, a drugged stupor, or a computer program. Just step gingerly past the sleeping dog on the path, ready to reveal that your quest isn't philosophical at all; it's just a rationale for evading your life.

These five tools are ways to avoid the exposure and potential humiliation of living an open and undisguised life. All have their role in a balanced life as well, but overused they all point in the same direction: away. The alternative, after all, is too daunting to face.

"Acting," said Rosalind Russell, "is standing up naked and turning *very slowly.*" So is living. But it's easy not to take part in the communal striptease. Just imagine my friend, with no drinks in the tank, getting up mid-party, lights turned up and music off, unbuttoning and pulling off the bodysuit, letting it fall to the floor. There would be nothing to joke about, no irony, no artificial abs shaded into his stomach. It would really be him, standing there, exposed. Some would disapprove, others would laugh.

Safer to clothe yourself in distance. Or, better still, to turn down the party invitation altogether.

PART FOUR

Navigating the Seas of Adulthood

One of the most jolting days of adulthood comes the first time you run out of toilet paper. Toilet paper, up until this point, always just existed. And now it's a finite resource, constantly in danger of extinction, that must be carefully tracked and monitored, like pandas.

— Kelly Williams Brown, *Adulting*

Ohhh, you may be thinking. You're reading this book too late. The ship to misery has sailed, and you missed it. Or you got on the wrong boat and have been sailing away from misery for years.

- Unimpressed with the appeals of childhood, you have left home, spurned the breast, stopped rebelling, and given up the futile quest to change your family.

- Too self-aware to buy into the messages from the culture, you have recognized that you are not so unique, that happiness is no impediment to action, that passions can be nurtured from a passing interest, that talent is no substitute for practice, and that confidence is a result of action, not a prerequisite for it.

- Conscious of the need to develop a self worth expressing, you have built your skills, risen above restrictive self-definitions, exposed yourself to the world (in a good way), and left at least a few marshmallows on the plate.

Disaster. Perhaps you are doomed to adulthood; to a lifetime of responsibility and fulfillment; to a world in which others look to you as someone who has her or his poop together. Is all truly lost?

Of course not.

You can spend years in the garage building a sailboat. Lay the keel, assemble the structure, fiberglass the hull, raise the mast, rig the sail. Roll it out into the water. Perfect. Seaworthy. Ready for adventure. Are you sure of success? Not on your life. Spin the compass, steer toward the rocks, and misery awaits.

Let's switch vehicles. Remember learning to ride a bike? Climb aboard, feet on pedals—and you cannot possibly remain upright if you are stationary. Pedal forward and you have to juggle both momentum and balance, neither of which you have mastered. You lean to the left, panic, overcorrect, and falter rightward. You swerve right, miss the balance point, and teeter left again. You strive for a balance that you never truly achieve. Cycling is an endless process of beginning to topple, recovering, and tipping again.

Life is similar. "Steady as she goes," they say. "Set your course and stick to it." But there are no steady courses. Every moment you are careening toward walls or over cliffs. Stay in bed and nothing gets done, keep walking and you're mowed down by traffic, keep eating and you bust buttons, keep working and you burn out. Stay on track—any track at all—and disaster awaits. Change, adjustment, correction—these are the only constants.

Most of the difficulties of life can be reduced to one of two states: too much of something or not enough. Money, sex, booze, work, downtime, screen time, nap time. We try to navigate between the extremes and, as with cycling, we tend to overshoot. Noticing ourselves too far to one side, we turn more sharply than necessary and become just as imbalanced in the other direction. Often more so. Overstimulated, we isolate. Overworked, we quit. Overfed, we fast. Starving, we stuff ourselves. Bored, we overextend. We careen from deficit to overdose. It doesn't matter which we choose. Misery lies to either side.

191

It's easy to avoid contentment, which takes a steadier hand, a clearer map, a gentler touch, and a taste for balance. Looking for misery? Just let go of the handlebars. It will find you.

In this section, then, let's go for the opposite of fine-tuning. Let's set our course for despair. Start the car, throw it in drive, and ram the garage wall. Step up to the skydive door, leap out, and never pull the rip cord. Point your bike downhill, close your eyes, and coast. Hop aboard, and let's set out for darker horizons.

Go with the Flow

Here's a paradox: to reach the goal of misery, it's useful to have no goals at all. Let's consider why.

Life comes with a guarantee: the more precisely you specify your destination, the less likely it is that you will wind up exactly there. The career will be unexpected. The spouse will be taller or shorter. The home will be laid out differently. The picket fence will be yellow, not white. Ask a dozen fifty-year-olds if they are squarely where they had planned to be, to the last decimal point, and none will say yes. They would not have anticipated a person like Chris, the accident of Max, the unexpected flowering of a taste for slam poetry.

So why bother planning? Knowing the world will change, knowing you can't see over the horizon of time, knowing that even your own self-knowledge is limited, what's the point? Better to relax, take what comes, and wait to see what fate tosses your way. Humans plan; God laughs. Sit on the couch today and every day. Let tomorrow take care of itself. Do this and you need never leave the apartment. Misery will be delivered to your door like a toxic pizza.

Of course, some effort will be involved. You'll have to ignore the fact that every achievement is built from multiple bricks of experience and preparation, that every successful relationship takes work done long before the partner is met, that distant destinations are reached by many steps. You'll need to suppress your knowledge that while no one arrives precisely where they had planned, they only got where they did by actually setting out on the journey—and for that they needed at least a tentative goal.

Let's step back a minute.

On the map, Barkley Sound looks like a giant has taken a bite out of Vancouver Island, leaving behind the hundred tiny crumbs of the Broken Islands. Kayak out beyond the outer islets and your view is of open Pacific, next stop Japan. It's tempting to stop paddling and gaze out at the blue. Peaceful. Gentle swells, when it's not raining. But what's that sound approaching from behind?

It's a lee shore. The prevailing wind is forever blowing eastward, pushing you inexorably to the surf-pounded rocks. Pause too long and you lose the boat, and maybe your life.

Out here the rules are simple. Enjoy it. Paddle under the sun. Camp out under the stars. Count the seals swimming alongside. Drink the wine you packed in the dry bags. But keep an eye on the far horizon for storm clouds. Know where you're heading for the night. And look behind you.

Life too is a lee shore. That couch is drifting, and that sound behind you is high water breaking on sharp rocks. Easy to think that by not moving, you're not moving. But you are. Cast onto the shoals of your fortieth birthday with no skills, no plans, no career, no accomplishments, no progress? Congratulations—that's misery.

In therapy, many of my depressed clients have explored misery quite exhaustively and are ready for an alternative. They're building toward a different frame of mind—toward mental health. Sometimes they wonder, though: What happens if they succeed? Mental health is fine, if you like that sort of thing. But what are they going to use it for? What mission are they on? What goals sit beyond the horizon of their cure?

Their quandary can be your brake pedal. No point in building a motorcycle you don't plan to ride, a house you don't want to live in, a path you have no intention of walking. Head to the recycling depot and drop off any goals you've already identified; maybe someone else will want them. Lighten your load of any thought for the future, and live only for the moment.

Even if you do want to achieve a few things, how do you decide between them? As we have discussed (see Lesson 21), the full list of skills and experiences is far too long to get through in just one lifetime. You have to pick and choose, and how do you do that?

True, some of them are pretty good bets. The ability to do basic arithmetic, unclog a toilet, or make a quesadilla? Those would likely prove useful no matter which path you take.

The rest are more arcane. Only dive shop owners need to know how to clean vomit out of regulators. No one needs to know how to operate every button on a television remote. So which items from the hundred-page menu should you select? It's hard to pack your suitcase if you're not sure where you're going.

If you're going to treat goals as cow pats and avoid soiling your espadrilles with them, it's best you know where they are so you can step around them. Consider seven of the primary realms of life.

- *Vocational.* Jobs you'd like, careers to pursue, components of work that are important to you (outdoors? social? prestigious? sustainable?).

- *Avocational.* Things you'd like to do that might not pay the rent, but fit your values or interests (photography? community theater? carpentry? teaching language skills to refugees?).

- *Contributory/spiritual.* Ways of using your skills or time to benefit others or explore your inner world (volunteering? philanthropy? advocacy? religious observance?).

- *Experiential.* Flavors from life's ice cream store that you would like to taste (bungee jumping? Nepal? communal living? being tasered?).

- *Social/familial.* Elements of life involving other people (marriage? kids? caring for parents? travel with friends?).

- *Educational.* Skills or knowledge that you'd like to acquire (magic tricks? first aid? Latin? tuba?).

- *Financial/ownership.* Goals related to money and things you might like to spend it on (get an electric unicycle? pay off student loans? buy a house? earn a certain salary?)

For maximum misery, keep each of these seven slots pristine and empty. Without a destination in mind, you can drive in ennui-inducing circles, bored by the ride and struck by its point-lessness. Perfect for the seeker of unhappiness. Tell yourself that you are being spontaneous. That you are living in the moment. That you are leaving room for the universe to tap you on the shoulder. Ignore the fact that it only seems to tap those holding a map.

In short, go with the flow. Keep the horizon close and never look beyond it. Do not ask where you will be in five years, or in ten. Do not invest in a future that might be derailed by an errant asteroid strike. Close your eyes, and let your kayak drift gently on the waves. No need to turn and look for the lee shore. It'll find you on its own.

Set Your Heart on the Stars

Living a goal-free life isn't the only route to misery. If this book has taught you anything, it should be that there are multiple descents into life's emotional valleys. So: to reach the gutter, aim for the stars.

Want to make films? Surpass Spielberg. Be an author? Outsell Rowling. Write music? Bypass Bach. Start a business? Leave Bezos, Bloomberg, and Buffet behind, choking on your dust. There's a name for the humble member of town council, for the journeyman electrician, for the efficient waiter, for the uniformed traffic cop, for the doting parent with an evening book-keeping practice, for the second in any field. *Failure.*

No point in playing the nickel slots. Go big or go home. No one ever entered the Olympics skating for silver.

In a world dominated by media, the high school teacher down the street pales in comparison with the celebrities you know best. Every morning you flip open the laptop and sip coffee with the stars, debate policy with presidents, chat business with billionaires, hash out strategy with heavies of the NHL, NBA, and NFL. These are your peers. Not the Little League coach at work, the realtor next door, the local weather guy across the alley. It is no longer sufficient to be a biggish fish in a small pond, because there are no small ponds. There is only the wide ocean, and winning means reaching the apex of the food chain. It's *Jaws* or nothing.

By this standard, we're all in luck. It isn't just you who has thus far failed and will almost certainly continue to fail for a lifetime. It's your family. Your friends. It's everyone you know. You swim in a school of mediocrities and failures, and despite moments of hyper-caffeinated grandeur, mostly you know the truth. You are vanishingly unlikely to meet your—or your culture's—standards of complete success. You too will be a failure in someone's eyes; most especially your own. If you get the job, you won't land the corner office. If you sign on with the cruise ship, you'll never own it. Become a chef; you'll never be Lagasse. Learn the violin, and Jascha Heifetz will mock you from the grave.

Doesn't matter. Demand that you reach your lofty goal anyway and resolve never to feel satisfied, never to be content, never to enjoy life until you get there. Ignore the fact that even vast and incontrovertible success usually fails to produce the satisfaction and self-assurance you covet. Churchill had depression. Tiger Woods flamed out more than once. Tina Fey, Tom Hanks, Kate Winslet, Ryan Reynolds, and many others describe feeling like imposters. Doesn't matter. Someone has to sit on the pointy bit of the pyramid. Why not you? Tell yourself that if you reach the golden throne, you, unlike all those others, will be content.

By framing existence as a race with a single winner, we pave a route that thousands have trod. Endlessly pursuing the big score, we neglect the prizes along the way. A friend of a friend has seized upon visionary scheme after visionary scheme (clean coal? blue-green algae? day trading? defunct mining town real estate?), and at age seventy continues in impoverished yet increasingly desperate pursuit as the clock ticks down. Be like him. In short: if you want misery, mistake grandiosity for ambition. There's nowhere to go but down.

But wait. Isn't aiming high supposed to be the road to greatness, not failure? In order to arrive at your destination, you have to know what it is, no? Keep your eye on the ball. Stay hungry. Never settle for second best. These are the culture's mantras of achievement.

Most high achievers, if they're honest, acknowledge that much of what happened in their lives was unplannable luck: the market upswing, the unexpected niche, the influential mentor, the chance meeting on the street. Meryl Streep didn't anticipate all her Oscars, Richard Branson didn't start out aiming for space, Bob Dylan wasn't targeting the Nobel. They paid attention to where they were, and to the next steps along the way. Their progress could never have been achieved without any notion of what they wanted in life. The road to the absolute pinnacle, though? Not something that could be mapped with any certainty.

But forget all that. Aim for the improbable peak anyway. It's a reliable road to misery for three reasons.

1. A focus on the apex of success will cast the rest of the journey into shadow. Any goal, from finding a spouse to becoming an accountant to winning the World Cup, involves dozens or even hundreds of small achievements along the way. Every hill climbed reveals a taller one still to be scaled. If twenty years hence you reach your ultimate goal, you will be a success only then, and a failure all the days leading up to it.

2. The golden glare of the achievement will blind you to the task at hand. Lost in reverie about the presidency, you will miss the filing deadline for town council candidates. Planning the marketing of your bestseller will crowd out the time for writing. Focused on leaping from the plane, you may neglect to buckle your parachute.

3. A laser focus on distant goals can sap motivation rather than building it. When you're thinking of the thousand rungs between you and your goal, any action taken today can seem trivial to the point of irrelevance. You will fail to reap the satisfactions en route. You won't notice the sunsets, smell the roses, hear the first scatterings of applause. Starved for pleasure, your interest will dry up long before you get to your destination.

I recently asked a young man who felt stuck in life what he wanted to be. A writer, he told me. I asked what he wrote.

Nothing, he said—no one had hired him. I gently pointed out that his first thousand pages would almost certainly never be published. It would take him years to experience the first flickers of prowess—and he would never master the craft of writing entirely, never feel completely assured that he was as good as he had once envisioned. Dreaming about his goal was preventing him from reaching it.

Follow his example. Dream big and dream far, and keep your eye on that distant and improbable ball. Focus so intently on that distant shore that you can't find the bridge leading there.

Keep Your Options Open

In Part Two, we reviewed how the culture shouts its mantras at us. *You can do anything you set your mind to. You can be anyone you want to be. The possibilities are endless.*

It was always a bit of a lie, of course. With your myopia, being an astronaut was out. Being born outside the country meant you could never be president. Episcopalianism ruled out becoming pope. The brackets around your potential, though, were genuinely wide.

Today, a vast array of options remains open, and this panoply of potential can seem like your primary source of wealth.

But there's a hitch. The moment you make a decision, you narrow the range.

- You cannot simultaneously study organic chemistry at Harvard and interpretive dance in Copenhagen.

- Accepting that placement on Wall Street rules out the dive shop in Belize.

- You can form a relationship with Joanne, but she doesn't want to share you with Curtis.

Every decision advances one of your options, but inevitably relinquishes many more. There are hundreds of college programs, thousands of career options, millions of people you might be with. Life is a multidimensional chessboard, but only one piece can be moved at a time, and only to a single square. Heading to London puts Cincinnati out of reach. Playing jazz in New Orleans means sayonara to soil ecology in Idaho. Making choices eats away at your freedom.

So conserve your options. Remain at the crossroads as long as you can. Make no decisions. Tell yourself that you cannot lose the game if you don't make a move.

The reason this is such a reliable avenue to misery is sitting right there beside the chessboard: the timer. It's not just by choosing that you lose choices. They vanish on their own as time ticks by.

One of the reasons the twenties pose such a challenge is that you get the first real inkling of narrowing possibilities. If you have not taken up sprinting by twenty-five, winning gold in the hundred meters is already off the menu. The distant walls of your life have shifted perceptibly inward. Maybe you never really aspired to be a champion figure skater, or a Junior Miss World, or a Mozart-ian piano prodigy. There's a difference, though, between not wanting something and having it taken from you without your permission.

This relentless winnowing of futures will only continue and accelerate: an early harbinger of your eventual extinction. Each alternative is a grain of sand in an hourglass. As you sit, options continually drip through it and away. There is no preserving them. One day, at thirty, you'll awaken and realize that no one will ever call you precocious again. It is too late to be a savant.

Also, if you look carefully you'll notice that most of what you think are options aren't actually free for the taking. They have prerequisites. Try to pick up game design; you need to have learned coding first, or drawing, or graphic art. Most of the options you hope to preserve depend on you having made earlier decisions—then and only then do they enter the realm of possibility.

- Drug and alcohol counseling? Unlikely until you've kicked your own habit.

- Wilderness guiding? You need to know avalanche rescue skills first.

- Molecular biology? Best get your high school certificate before you even think about it.

Making decisions removes some options from the table, but places others within range. The fear of wasting time headed down a blind alley is a prime barrier to decision making, and a greased ramp to misery. Dwell on the chance that any choice you make will prove to be the wrong one. *What if I discover that I don't actually like ornithology, or welding, or spelunking?* Could happen. Ruminating on the prospect is a great way to prevent yourself from taking action.

Ignore the fact that, having made a choice, you would have some experience, whereas remaining stationary provides none. Many of these apparent misfires can themselves prove strangely useful in a way that could never have been predicted.

- A knowledge of birds could have helped with the environmental impact assessments for the renewable energy company you might have had.

- Your welding certificate would have boosted your résumé with the Coast Guard.

- Your cave explorations, had you made them, would impart confidence when tunneling through law school.

To be sure, some paths do turn out to be dead ends. Most people stuff a few cards up their sleeves that never prove useful, or never as anything more than dinner conversation. Curb your enthusiasm by dwelling on the potential pointlessness of any move you might make.

Putting off decisions, of course, is itself a decision. Waiting for inspiration or clarity is a decision to pass time with nothing to show as a result. So set up camp at the crossroads and huddle there in your tent, clutching your options tightly to your chest.

It's easy to win the game of misery. When it's your turn, you don't have to decide what to do. Just pass. And pass. And pass.

Avoid Risk

Are you longing for misery, yet fearful of the leap into the unknown? No problem. Take no chances. Spend your life dancing frantically away from extremely low-probability threats.

Consider: the human species has come to dominate our planet (for better or worse) not because we are stronger or larger than any other animal, but because evolution has made us adaptable. Living without the benefits of modern technology, ancient humans managed to populate the world's deserts, mountains, plains, islands, jungles, and arctic, primarily by virtue of an intensely convoluted and interconnected brain. Of the brain's many functions, one has done far more to ensure our proliferation than any other: the ability to solve problems.

In order to solve a problem, of course, you have to recognize that it exists. You have to pay attention to bad omens; think about the threats. Consequently, we have a biologically driven bias to detect the dangerous over the safe, the unsatisfactory over the sufficient, and the perilous over the peaceful. Given a dozen signs of safety and a single hint of a lurking predator, the survival imperative has made us focus on the one at the expense of the many. For us, misery isn't an aspiration. It's an evolutionary adaptation.

We have brought this threat-seeking brain into a modern setting created specifically to keep us safe and comfy. Our understimulated danger detectors have compensated by ratcheting up their sensitivity, with the result that most of us magnify small hazards and overpredict catastrophe. The surest way to attract a human being's attention is with danger messages, a fact noticed and utilized by advertisers, twenty-four-hour news networks, politicians, fanatics, and other would-be influencers.

In the modern world, there are, to be sure, genuine problems with which we have to contend. Climate change is a significant threat to global stability and the carrying capacity of the planet. Authoritarian leadership, itself enabled by fear, can erode the values and lives of even those supporting it. A high-calorie diet and low-activity lifestyle may lull couch-dwellers into early graves. Not all is well in suburbia.

Our eyes are often drawn away from these real threats, however, to less-apocalyptic hazards that in past decades might have been dismissed.

- Recommend that a friend leave their cell phone at home when embarking on a drive through the countryside. Watch their eyebrows lift in alarm at the thought of snowdrifts, serial killers, and breakdowns, with no immediate recourse to 911.

- Suggest an evening walk through the city and count the milliseconds before receiving a flat refusal. Anyone doing so would surely be killed in no time.

- Let the kids make their own way to school, then wait for the knock on the door from irate neighbors or Children's Services. Those who, decades earlier, safely walked to school alone will have forgotten they ever did so.

Can you see yourself in these examples? If so, justify your aversion by pointing to the ambiguities in the world. In childhood, all was clear. You learned absolute truth after absolute truth. Poodles are dogs. Not all dogs are poodles. The Tooth Fairy exists. The number 15 bus goes downtown. Poison ivy makes poor toilet paper. Simple.

But this clarity diminishes with age. You think that you finally understand life, then realize that much cannot be known, little is certain, and once-solid facts change. Dietary fat will kill you. Dietary fat is essential. Misery grows in the cracks of ambiguity, and demanding certainty of the world only provides the fertilizer.

Some days you know how things are going to go. You have the same breakfast as usual, ride the same transit, sit at the same desk, and spend your evening the way you have a thousand times before. If life is a highway, most days are clear, open stretches with the road ahead plainly visible. Every so often, though, we can't see very far. The road leads into a dark tunnel, and we don't know what will appear on the other side.

The miserable strategy is to see these tunnels as brick walls and avoid them. Take the lack of clarity as a sign not to go there. To this end: four recommendations.

- *Run from failure.* Short-term, failure is pretty good at producing unhappiness. For truly lasting misery, however, don't try anything new. If you do happen to stray from your established path, give up at the first hint of trouble. Your life will spiral inward to the activities with which you are comfortable, you will never achieve anything, and you can make yourself miserable dwelling on your disappointment.

- *Play it safe.* Minimize your exposure to all unpleasant possibilities. Ski lifts break down. Planes crash. Divers drown or are eaten by sharks. Readers get paper cuts. Never adventure. There is a happy medium, of course, between sensible caution and foolhardiness. Avoid this. Err on the side of certainty instead. Don't go to a restaurant unless you know the menu; don't attend a job interview unless it's certain you will be hired.

- *Procrastinate.* Ordeals that you eventually have to face—like writing essays, or repairing plumbing, or getting blood tests, or mowing the lawn—should be put off to maximize the agony. You'll still have the discomfort of the task, but to this you can add the guilt and dread of the anticipation. Stand shivering at the edge of the chilly pool for as long as you can. You'll feel the shock of the water just as much—or perhaps even more—than if you had leapt right in.

- *Avoid getting your heart broken.* It hurts a lot, so why risk it? You will only know you can survive being dumped after you've come out the other side, and until then the uncertainty is surely too much to face. Don't put your heart on the line. Don't show your true self. Don't get emotionally attached. Tell yourself you're not ready. The truth is, you'll never be ready, and you'll get steadily less ready and more fearful the longer you avoid it.

And here we are again: long-term pain produced in the simplest way possible—by the pursuit of short-term comfort. It's always easy to put off the risks, the gambles, the possibilities of failure until tomorrow, and tomorrow, and tomorrow. The happier among us weigh the odds, calculate the benefits and losses, and take leaps into the unknown.

It's so much easier to stand shivering on the shore.

Ignore Distant Payoffs

As tempting as it is to stay on the couch, every so often we are forced into a decision about what to do next with our lives. An opportunity saunters by and we have to figure out whether to grab hold or let it pass.

To minimize the risk of happiness, always base your choice on the immediate outcome, not the eventual possibility.

Let me explain with an example.

Recently a friend of mine was offered a contract to teach performance skills to a group of scientists at a tony retreat center in the mountains. It would involve canceling his existing commitments, preparing three presentations from scratch, flying there the day before, and teaching a long, exhausting day before flying home again that evening—all for a fee that, while high, wouldn't pay for the days of prep time the program would take him.

"Is it worth it?" he asked.

The answer was obvious: of course not. He could make more money with less stress by maintaining his regular vocal training business and taking on a few more clients. In his own studio he knew what he was doing, and he wouldn't be setting himself up for disappointment, humiliation, lost baggage, and getting mounted by a horny moose.

If he looked at it over the longer term, however, the answer was different. He'd been wanting to do large-scale workshops for years, and they were more remunerative than his usual gig—at least once he had the tools in the bag. The preparation he'd do for this one contract would mean developing a series of "products" that he could sell over and over again—and he would be getting paid to do it. If he was serious about this next step in his career, the answer was clear: sign on.

My friend was faced with a situation that recurs often in people's lives and careers. The immediate benefit of a task simply cannot justify the cost in terms of the time, money, or effort involved. Future payoffs from the same effort are often uncertain or unforeseeable. We may not have any idea how learning to juggle, scuba dive, or install drywall could prove useful in the future—and they may not. The conservative approach is to take intangible prospective gains off the table when making your decision. This keeps you right where you are, and if you're dissatisfied you will perpetuate your misery.

Making an investment in time or effort in the present is like installing a glitter bomb in your future—it could go off at any time and propel you into a life for which you haven't planned. This is something to avoid.

I objected strenuously in high school when my father insisted I take typing. I was perfectly satisfied with my two-finger method.

He pointed out that it would be useful when writing essays. I replied that most of my assignments didn't have to be typed anyway, and that it was a waste to spend an entire term learning a skill that might only speed me up a little in the future.

I lost the argument and signed up for typing. On typewriters. Which, in case you haven't noticed, no longer exist. I was resentful of my father for pushing me around, and angry at myself for caving in so easily. Outcome: of all the high school courses I took, typing paid off the most.

Another example: in my final undergraduate year I had the chance to work in the lab of cognitive scientist Anne Treisman, as a lowly lab technician doing research in an area I already suspected I didn't want to pursue. Pretty dull work, much of it, and lower paying than some of my alternatives. I could have gone back to my summer job operating a packaging machine, shipping out marine hardware and blissfully drinking beer every Friday on the loading dock.

Fear of that future got the better of me. I spent much of my twenty-first year coloring index cards with felt pens, then flipping them in and out of a tachistoscope for bored research volunteers. *Press the button if you see a green H.*

Even though I missed the beer, the path to misery, I see now, would have been to remain on the loading dock. Turns out I liked both coloring and the lab's many margarita parties. Plus, my eventual graduate supervisor accepted my application largely on the basis of my work with Treisman, and a year later she added me as a coauthor on a study that became a touchstone in the field of attention.[16]

The research exposure solidified my interest in psychology and made me (slightly) less clueless with my own lab work later on. I published more papers than I would have otherwise, which increased my confidence in writing. That one decision to take the job in the lab influenced the rest of my life. I'd almost missed it, and I would have if I'd made my decision based on the job's hourly rate.

Here are some examples of activities that run the risk of eventual payoffs that make misery harder to sustain:

- Saving money

- Developing skills (languages, sports, public speaking, cooking)

- Volunteer work

- Creating personal habits (making the bed, cleaning up, being on time)

- Remembering friends' birthdays

- Travel

"Yes," it's tempting to say, "but I have so little time and money in my twenties that it's hard to spare any for the future. I'll invest in myself later, when I'm older and richer."

Keep telling yourself this. You can't afford it. Sneer at those who yammer about "the path not taken." How do they know it doesn't lead over a cliff?

To be miserable, focus on the immediate frame. If working at a dead-end job pays a dollar more an hour than a job where you'll learn something valuable, take it. Do your accounting—and decision making—based on clearly visible present outcomes, not on the hypothetical and impossible-to-predict future.

Let the Money Worry About Itself

Lackadaisical money management is an express train to misery. It has regular departures and no stops along the way, though admittedly the ticket price is exorbitant.

If you're a billionaire, of course, lousy financial judgment may not make much difference to your daily comfort. You might stress out about losing $100 million, but you'd still be able to afford dinner and a movie. The opportunities for utter desolation are a bit limited.

In our twenties, though, most of us don't have billions. You needn't fret over whether to take the Ferrari or the McLaren to the grocery store, or wonder whether a superyacht is too extravagant. It may be challenging enough to scrape together bus fare. You can find yourself living uncomfortably close to the edge of your personal financial cliff, loose pebbles crumbling into the void below. You're trying to buy a bed to lift the mattress off the floor, retain enough funds to pay the rent, get something into a savings account, and maybe build up a credit rating. More than once in my twenties I went through the couch cushions looking

for money to fund a night at the pub. A friend of mine at graduate school sold her record collection for a bag of rice.

To feel truly wretched, however, you don't have to be a starving student. As your income rises you can accumulate bigger and
bigger bills that make the cliff higher and the rocks at the bottom
pointier. Don't bother trying to balance the amount dripping
from the money tap and the amount draining down the plughole.
If you can afford a million-dollar home, mortgage your soul for
five times that. If you have the means for a ski condo, buy a
chalet instead. If you're flush with money, head to Vegas and
flush it away.

Few strategies are more effective at promoting misery than
debt and overspending, because few enlist the help of so many
invested parties (the government, your landlord, the credit card
company, the bank) who will lend a hand turning the screws.
How can you maximize the effects? Let me count the ways.

1. Don't pay your taxes. No one has as long a memory, as
   many resources, or as much inclination to expend huge
   effort reclaiming a small debt as the government does. It
   may seem inconceivable that you would let spring slide
   by without filing a tax return, but thousands—or millions—do. Having done it once, it's easier the second
   time and easier still the tenth, especially given the
   added fear that filing for the current year will remind

them of your existence over the preceding decade and spark an investigation.

2. Equate credit with money. Your credit line—or the limit on your bank card—is easy to reconceptualize as a pile of money sitting there waiting for you to spend it. Once you do, the credit card company becomes your lord and master. This is especially true if you go over the amount you can conceivably repay at the end of the month. They call you the cardholder but it's not a card, it's a collar—and they're the ones holding your leash.

3. Spend based on how much you should be earning, or believe you soon will be earning, not on how much you actually make. "Hey, by next spring I'll be paid $50,000, so I can manage $3,000 on a bender in Mexico." Actually, you only make whatever's left over after your monthly expenses and taxes, which is a lot less than you might think, and a lot can happen between now and next spring.

4. Assume your inaugural apartment has to be ready in case *Architectural Digest*, ZZ Top, or Jennifer Lawrence pop by for a photo shoot. They won't. But furnish it to impress anyway. The anxiety about an empty bank account will exceed the calming influence of a $2,500 set of chairs.

So how do you decide where to put your money?

- For misery, base your spending on what feels tempting. Every marketer and advertiser is trying to help you with this by promising a little bit of paradise should you open your wallet for them. That club outfit / TV / expensive dinner / fancy car / back-waxing seems like it's just calling out to you, but it'll shut up the moment you buy it and you can settle in for a long visit with regret.

- For happiness, ask yourself what has actually proven satisfying in the past. Look around at the possessions and experiences you've already paid for (or the last twenty items on your credit card bill) and ask yourself how happy you are to have them instead of the money they cost. The past is a clearer guide to satisfaction than your gut will ever be.

It's fashionable to say that consumerism is not the path to happiness. It would perhaps be more accurate to say that it isn't the only or most direct route. Most of us can identify possessions that have contributed to ongoing life satisfaction or to a storehouse of valued memories. The bicycle, the concert ticket, the kitchen pots, the cabin weekend with friends, the gym membership, the flannel sheets.

Money sunk into an object, however, is transformed into that object alone. Money kept as money retains its potential to become any object in the marketplace. It is a cushion, a security blanket, an insurance policy against future adversity. But to have it takes careful attention and effective money management skills, with which no one is born. To be miserable, ensure that you never acquire these.

Money does not take care of itself. And it never worries on anyone's behalf. It has you for that.

Take Your Body for Granted

New cars are great. Not much goes wrong and you can drive them hard without worrying. Two days on the highway? No problem. Off-road camping? Easy. Moving your friend's weight set? Piece of cake. If you ignore basic maintenance, things can still go wrong—and you'll pay in the long run. But short term, you're in the clear.

A just-past-puberty body, given enough time for the gaps to fill in, is similar. In your twenties you have a frame that'll take a lot of abuse and spring back. Like a car, you still have to do some maintenance. Just because bad stuff (spinal cord injury, HIV infection, type 2 diabetes) hasn't happened yet doesn't mean it can't. Without a little extra care and attention you may be on the road to misery without half trying. Chronic health problems may wait to appear until your thirties or beyond, but the sense of the clock ticking and payback time approaching will be a drag on your mood long before karma comes knocking at the door.

I routinely assess people who are forty and miserable. Every client is a detective story. Some are like the most convoluted

Agatha Christie plots. Others are more like Two-Minute Mysteries.

"How do you spend an average day?"

"At work I mostly sit in front of a screen, then I drive home, eat a burger and fries for dinner, and watch TV with a few beers."

Ah. I point out that their existence sounds like a recipe for lousy mental health.

"Yeah," they'll often say. "But I did the same when I was younger and I felt fine."

Yup. New car. In their twenties, some people can do practically anything to their bodies, experience no immediate physical consequences, and feel emotionally more or less well. Random sleep cycle, sedentary lifestyle, lousy diet, 90 percent of the day spent staring at screens, binge-drinking, isolation, the works. The body doesn't completely fall apart, and the mind, while not thrilled, hangs on.

Later on, the effect is more immediate. Live exactly the same way at thirty-five, at forty-five, at fifty-five, and things don't go so well. Take a middle-aged car and drive it aggressively down jolting roads, loaded to the max, old oil clogging the engine, and it's not going to last long. The baseline mood at forty—with no maintenance, no exercise, no dietary adjustment, no stability, and no social life—is misery.

This doesn't mean that buoyancy and resilience are no longer attainable. They are. I feel better now, for example, than I ever did in my twenties, and research suggests that for most people life satisfaction rises from the mid-forties onward.

Not to worry, however. Contentment won't invade your life without a deliberate effort on your part. Those who want happiness lever themselves off the emotional floor by making their body move, as it was designed to, and by giving it the right fuel, getting enough sleep, supplementing nutrients where necessary, treating friendships as mandatory rather than optional, taking breaks, and calibrating the dose of toxins (like alcohol) they pour down the hatch. They pay attention to their knees, they watch their waist size, they preserve their lungs by not smoking, they progressively cut out high-calorie, low-nutrition foods, and if they're male they occasionally let their physician stick her finger up their butt.

It's possible that you can ignore all this and still not become miserable. Maybe you're one of those twenty-five-year-olds who can eat anything and not inflate like a balloon or dissolve your own esophagus with stomach acid. No need to worry. This won't last. At age twenty-eight or twenty-nine you'll notice this start to change.

- Having worn the same size since high school, you suddenly discover you need the next one up.

- Having had a few beers every night for a decade without trouble, you start waking up with hangovers.

- Having gone since puberty without seeing a doctor, you undergo a series of blood tests that reveal high blood pressure and off-the-charts cholesterol.

All this is only the beginning, unless you pay attention. It's true that when the elderly are asked for sage advice for the young, "Take care of your teeth" is one of the first things they say.

Part of the problem is the way we speak. "My body." As if it's something other than you. "My transit card." "My bath mat." "My vintage *Seinfeld* T-shirt." A human being saying that he or she has a body is like a car saying that it has a car. Doing so suggests a fundamental misunderstanding of the relationship.

Your body is you. Neglect it and you neglect yourself. Not your digestion, not your fingernails, not your sunburned skin, not your slackening endurance, not your slowing circulation. You. You needn't decorate it with makeup or hundred-dollar haircuts or purely decorative muscle mass if that doesn't suit you. But make no mistake: its functioning is your functioning. You and your canister are one.

As so often seems to be the case, misery is easy to reach. It's the main route, the superhighway, the hyperspace bypass. Eat what's advertised, watch the screens around you, use the escalator, lift heavy things any way you like, and avoid boring maintenance. You'll eventually glide effortlessly into unhappiness.

It's the opposite path, that disused off-ramp leading strenuously uphill toward happiness, that takes effort.

Focus on What You Lack

Take a look at that kombucha you've been drinking. Half full or half empty? If you want to be unhappy, you know what to do.

"I want it all" isn't just an old Queen tune. It's the unstated tagline of three-quarters of the advertising you see.

But of course, you will never have it all. If, somehow, you were to get it all, you wouldn't have room to store it anyway. There's only so much space, only so much time, only so many friends to juggle, only so many lovers who will fit in your bed, and you only have so much energy. If you had it all you'd have no room to move.

So there will always be two categories in your life: what you have, and what you don't. The latter is the larger—and all the more so early in life when we have had little time to accumulate history, skills, experience, possessions, and wealth. This doesn't change much, though: the glass will always be five-eighths or nine-tenths empty, not half.

Look at me. No yacht, no ski chalet, no private jet, no mansion, no hole in one (indeed, no golf clubs), no idea how to keep a peach tree alive, no plumbing skills to speak of, and no clue how to make chicken masala. It's looking like I'll go to the grave not knowing how to catch a pop fly, to boot.

This kind of perspective affords all of us a grand opportunity for disappointment. In my case, though, I haven't actually set my heart on most of what I lack—apart from the peach thing. So I'm reasonably content with whatever water I find in my glass. Ignore me, though. I just write about this quest for misery; I'm not actually on it.

Our mood does not depend, for the most part, on whether or not our life has deficits. It will always have deficits. Instead, it depends most on where we place our attention. If you focus on what you have—something no force in society encourages you to do—you may experience a sense of gratitude and abundance. If you focus on what you lack, precisely the same life will seem pathetic and poverty-stricken.

You can do this no matter what your actual circumstances are like:

- If you are tall, lament your disqualification as a jockey; if you are short, wish for a basketball scholarship.

- If others compliment your looks, regret that they cannot see the fine soul within; if they remark upon your generosity, attribute this to your homeliness.

- If you pilot Dreamliners, miss the adventure of bush planes; if you fly Twin Otters, long for the stability of an airline job.

Give it a shot. Think of something in your life that you are quite pleased about: your math grades, your guitar chops, the friendship that's going well, the great side table you bought last month, the weekend getaway you've booked next month, the music of Beethoven and Lady Gaga. Do this for two minutes and notice the feeling that develops.

Now think of your lousy grades in English, your utter inability to spike a volleyball, the friend who just moved to Tonga, the big-box store blighting your neighborhood. Concentrate on everything you lack—the butterfly collecting you no longer do with your friend, the dining table you can't afford, the Europe trip that's out of reach, the high school love affair that fizzled, the football career ended by a knee injury, the house swallowed by a sinkhole, the pet made impractical by allergies. Dwell on bereftness, and make these deficits your fault, your doing, the products of your inadequacy.

Two minutes. Notice the feeling.

You have the same life in both cases. The emotions you feel differ depending on where you place your attention. Your personal glass may not be empty, but it will never be entirely full either. There will always be a void on which you can focus.

When practicing this technique in everyday life, emphasize the deficits that cannot be overcome. It's no good mooning over that car in the sales lot if you have the money to buy it. That will only give you the pleasantly addictive hunger for acquisition.

Instead, lament the fact that you were not born richer, or into a different country, or with a different complexion, or with naturally aligned teeth. Mourn being adopted by a poor family, or having no siblings, or too many, or having an unstable parent. Dwell on the crushes that never returned your love, the jobs you were never given, the languages you never learned, the words you never spoke to people now deceased.

If you're going to bang your head against a wall, make it a hard one. We don't want rubber. We want stone.

Practice Mindlessness

Imagine that on a table in front of you sit three bowls, a pair of scissors, and a spool of film. Each frame of the film represents a single moment of your day. Cut off a frame and hold it up to the light. In that moment, where is your mind?

- If you are dwelling on the past—nursing old resentments, cataloging your regrets, recalling your humiliations, or enjoying memories of times gone by—place the frame in the bowl to your left.

- If you are contemplating the future—fearing disaster, daydreaming about success, anticipating next week's concert, planning your year, or dreading humiliation—place the frame in the bowl to your right.

- If your mind is settled on the immediate present—the seat beneath you, the movement in your visual field, the conversation with a friend, the words you are reading, the food you are preparing—place the frame in the bowl in the center.

Keep going. Look at the frame, notice where your mind is, drop it into a bowl. Do a whole day; a week if you're patient. Then look.

Which bowl has the most frames? Which has the fewest?

When I ask this question at conferences, the imagined bowls to the left and right usually vie for supremacy, overflowing onto the table and down to the floor. The center bowl, containing the moments in which you were focused on the present, almost always lags behind.

All of the bowls are important, no matter which direction on the satisfaction superhighway you choose.

- Happiness? You can learn from the past, remembering your pratfalls so you can avoid them next time, recalling which restaurant had that great salsa, or reminding yourself of the consequences of forgetting your partner's birthday. You can also plan for the future, anticipate risks, purchase tickets for the festival next month, study for the exam, go to bed to be fresh for tomorrow's run, and weigh your career options.

- Misery? Recall your mistakes, inventory your losses, replay the insults, and lament the missed opportunities, highlighting every disappointment and every

joy no longer available. Look ahead to disillusionment, to being found out, to illness, to your eventual extinction, to sagging skin, to root canal
surgery as yet unneeded.

But past and future are, in the end, both illusory. The past is
gone. The future does not exist and cannot be known until it
arrives. Only the present is real.

The present is your life. It is also the fulcrum of existence.
You cannot change the past or manipulate events a month from
now. You can only change what you are doing right now, in this
moment. It is the one lever of control you have over your life.

If the goal is misery, the mission is obvious. Leave the lever
alone. Avoid the middle bowl entirely. Spend all your time locked
in the past, fantasizing about the future, or shuttling from one to
the other. Not only will you inactivate whatever power you may
have, but you will eliminate most pleasure as well.

Unconvinced? Indulge me. Sort through the bowl of the
past for a moment, and find three good memories. Seriously. Try
it. What could it hurt?

Now: In those moments, were you anticipating something
from the future? Remembering something further back? Or
having an actual experience in what was then the now?

If you're like most people, virtually all of the treasured
moments in your life were times when you were fully present.

Gazing out at the ocean. Dancing. Cycling down a mountain trail. Running toward someone in the airport arrivals area. Being handed your license, your degree, your ring, your first paycheck, your citizenship papers, your baby, your freedom. To be truly miserable, it is these moments you must minimize or prevent.

If, by chance, you find yourself dwelling in the present, all is not lost. Toil in online game worlds. Watch actors playing out fictional scripts on video, or having sex before the cameras. Envy the hypothetical lives of your peers across town. Your mind will be on the imaginary present. Those race cars are just pixels, those television characters are just actors, those Internet posts originated a thousand miles away, those naked athletes will never know you, love you, or gaze into your eyes. They exist in the presentless present; the absent present.

But the times you seized the day, acted on a decision, marked a ballot, sat in the sun, climbed a mountain, tasted wonderful food, clung to an inner tube in a river, laughed with friends, studied for that exam, got on that plane, conquered that fear, made that speech, and said yes to your life? Then you were in the present. The present present. The real-life present. Not a memory; not a fantasy; not a distraction. Your life.

For misery, then, skip the next decade altogether. Play home movies of the past. Construct fantasies of the future. You will build no storehouse of satisfaction, no toolbox of skills, no foundation for the future. Your present will lack lasting interest, and you will lay the groundwork not only for this decade, but for all the decades to come. Practice the avoidance of the middle bowl until you have become adept—a black belt in the art of absence. The invisible man. The invisible woman. A contract killer of time.

The alternative? You'd have to contemplate that most vague of all contemporary terms: mindfulness. Which is, at its core, simply the art of residing for a little bit more of each day in that middle bowl. Not just in meditation, which is mostly a rehearsal for the continuation and practice of presence in the rest of life. Greater mindfulness doesn't prevent learning from the past or planning for the future; it simply allows the levers to be worked in the only place where they exist.

The present is your life. The ability to remain in it is the ability to have a life and influence how it goes. Not your cup of tea, surely.

Better to cultivate mindlessness. Look at those bowls again, to the left and right. Dive in and lose yourself in the frames.

Do It All Yourself

In Homer's *Odyssey*, the goddess Athena appears in the guise of Mentor, an old family friend, to Odysseus's son Telemachus. Mentor advises him to stop moping around, stand up to the guys hitting on his mother, and track down Dad, who has managed to get lost on his way home from Troy.

Twenty-eight hundred years pass, and suddenly mentorship is all the rage. Ignore this fashion, lest you be derailed from misery into fulfillment.

It's not like unrequested advice is anything new. Childhood is one long series of lectures from the world about what to do, when to do it, and how to think. Wipe your mouth. Stand up straight. Tie a double knot. Buckle up. Shoes come after socks. No, you can't ride on the hood. Keep stirring the béchamel. Call for a ride if you're drunk. Spermicide is not for oral use.

We long to graduate from the endless roster of teachers telling us how to live, trying to mold us into their own image, and taking out their red pen to circle every point where we have deviated from their vision for us.

So do it. Go it alone. Turn off the fire hose of advice directed your way. You're an adult. Stop getting bossed around. Stand on your own two feet. If someone older, more experienced, and more seasoned leans in to whisper a suggestion, rebuff them. You know what you're doing.

And hey—why do they want to help you anyway? There must be something in it for them. Turn away, plug your ears, and protect yourself.

Anyway, isn't that what people do? They select a school, weigh career options, decide whether to marry or have kids, and pick out a place to live, and you seldom catch them listening to a mentor. Most of these things aren't rocket science—not even (as a friend in the field tells me) rocket science itself.

So do it yourself. Pretend you are skiing virgin snow. Fresh tracks, no history. Imagine that no one has ever explored the territory you're entering.

At any rate, if someone *has* been here before—invented calculus, rebuilt a carburetor, created a business, wooed a partner—then obviously it's doable. You should be able to follow the same reasoning and work it out for yourself. If they can do it, you can do it. Stop looking for help.

This solo stance sounds suspiciously like adult independence, like maturity. How often do James Bond, Princess Leia, or Ethan Hunt stop and ask for directions? Never. Could their self-directed style really be a route to misery?

Yes.

When I started my private psychotherapy practice I was struck, again and again, by a sense of inadequacy. How do you negotiate with prospective landlords, manage financial records, soundproof a consulting room, set up the ground rules for associates, decide whether to incorporate, handle unpaid bills, write a practice announcement, and ensure you are not inadvertently avoiding taxes?

During my training, no one had ever told me any of these things. The implication was clear, at least to me: this is all so straightforward that there is no need to teach it. Any fool can do it.

It felt dangerous to reveal to others my lack of what must surely be common sense, so I shut my mouth and did what I felt certain every new business owner must do. I made it up. Then I discovered—a day later, a month later, four years later—that I had made mistake after mistake, boldly going where no one was stupid enough to go before.

It's hard to keep secrets forever. Hanging out with other therapists, I heard about their screwups and would share some of mine. What should perhaps have been obvious from the start became so gradually: none of us had known what we were doing at first. But if I had asked someone with prior experience what to do, none of this unhappiness would have been possible. With a strategy of standing on my own two feet I successfully created misery after misery, failure after failure.

Are you facing current challenges? One option is to shut yourself away and surf the Net for solutions. Another is to reveal your ignorance and ask someone for help. But in a cutthroat world of competition, why would anyone want to hand you an advantage?

I began this book with a discussion of Erik Erikson's life-stage theory. Leap, for a moment, past the twenties to midlife, a time when Erikson argues that most people experience an internal tug of war between two poles, pitting shrinkage against growth.

- *Stagnation:* a sense that one is becalmed in the doldrums of an unproductive existence, irrelevant and fading into obscurity.

- *Generativity:* a desire to pass on one's knowledge, skills, and resources for the welfare of other individuals and society as a whole.

Generativity sounds like a charitable act on the part of those who indulge in it. It isn't. Erikson framed it as a kind of psychological imperative—the kind of thing that sends salmon charging up raging rivers to spawn after a leisurely life at sea. It is a strange and unique sort of transaction, because the doing of a thing for the recipient *is* the payment for the giver. There is no other payback required or sought.

At the threshold of adulthood, I did not believe in this stage. People further down the road than I was wanted to help me out, but I thought they wanted either to steal my ideas or get into my pants. Little did I know—my ideas weren't so great, and my pants, judging from old photos, weren't as alluring as I had imagined.

All along, I was surrounded by outstretched hands, ready to give me a boost upward, but I was too proud to grab hold.

Want misery? Want to slow down your progress and smell the toadstools? Follow my example. View those hands with suspicion, and slap them away.

"All by myself" isn't just a Celine Dion cover song. It's the name of the streetcar you should jump aboard.

Turnabout

The trick is what one emphasizes. We either make ourselves miserable, or we make ourselves happy. The amount of work is the same.

—*Carlos Castaneda*

Ce que tu fuis te poursuit, ce à quoi tu fais face s'efface.
(What you flee pursues you; what you face fades away.)

—*Quebecois saying*

There. Forty lessons. Are we done yet? Have we exhausted the possibilities?

Hardly.

I've spent decades sitting in a chair listening to stories of how life goes wrong. The list seems endless. Misery lies in a valley of a thousand waterfalls, each torrent a different and rocky descent.

Life is often hard. Many of my clients—and many of my friends—have gone through some of the most shockingly awful and unpredictable experiences. The suicides of siblings. The cancers of children. Missing people who turned up dead, or married to other people and raising other families. Being disowned by parents. Watching businesses fail, bombs drop, and communities burn.

Unhappiness is really not so difficult to achieve. But we can always contribute to the cruelties of fate and make it worse.

THE SUBDIVISIONS OF MISERY

As discussed at the outset of our journey, the causes of misery fall into two categories. Column A comprises the negative influences on mood and life that are outside our control. Deaths, disasters, economic meltdowns, genetic anomalies, the accident of birth into a particular family/nation/culture/moment of history; the consequences of systemic racism, sexism, and the various societal phobias. We can do a little about some of these— voting, speaking up, donating to medical research, social justice activism—but we can't single-handedly eradicate them. We still have to cope with their impact.

It's tempting to attribute all of our misery to Column A and shout, "Not my fault! I didn't ask for this! None of my doing!"

Along with the absolution this provides, however, comes the helplessness. Nothing you could have done. Nothing you can do now to resolve it. No way to prevent it from happening again. You are a pinball doomed forever to be paddled by fate.

We all have some Column A in our lives. But we also have Column B: the factors over which we have at least a little influence. They are dance numbers requiring us to tango along, or at least shuffle our feet. Eating junk food, getting no exercise, vegetating endlessly in front of screens, sitting alone waiting to feel a surge of motivation or confidence or self-esteem.

The forty lessons of this book are all in Column B. There's no point in saying that an asteroid strike can make you miserable. You are not the master of the cosmos. The levers you can reach, the levers discussed here, are all on the B-side.

Column B also includes your reactions to the Column A calamities beyond your control. Do you cope with a facial burn by hiding yourself away or forcing yourself out? When your company goes bankrupt, do you shift gears and change direction or retreat to the couch and TV? Do you rage impotently about election results or do you campaign for voter registration?

So which is the bigger influence in your life, A or B?

Answer: it doesn't matter. B is all you've got to work with.

Circumstance, in the guise of Column A, may impose brackets around aspects of your life, but your position within that range depends mostly on your choices. Do you want to rise to the ceiling (which may prove higher than it first appears) or sink to the basement (which may be lower than you ever imagined)? There are many who have survived startling and unjust adversity who are among the world's happiest people. There are many living in great privilege who have difficulty making it through their day. Column B does more to determine emotional state than Column A, for the vast majority of people.

THE BASEMENT AND THE MINEFIELD

It's late. Why are you still reading? Unless you have been very lucky indeed, you already know how to be miserable, and if you've had a taste of that particular flavor of ice cream you're not going to ask for another scoop.

Let's go back to where we started: the basement of a psychiatric hospital, long past winter sunset. The people around the table in our post-hospitalization therapy groups didn't need to learn how to be miserable either. They already knew. That was the price of their admission.

In the process of identifying how they might make themselves worse, they could see what they were already doing toward that end. Finding the road from happiness to misery, they could begin edging right rather than left, and do the opposite of what their instincts might tell them.

You don't want to be miserable any more than they did, or than I do. It'll happen anyway, at times, but there's no need to prolong it or make it worse. You're looking for the peaks, not the valleys. But walk blithely along with your eyes on the mountain-tops and you'll stumble into some ravines along the way. We wind up at river bottom not because we want to be there, but because we miss the hazards, fall into creeks, lose our footing on tilted snowfields, and walk blindly over bluffs. You need a guide to the pitfalls, not the vistas.

The decade of the twenties is supposed to be terrific. You're allegedly in your prime and the world is your PlayStation. It's tempting to think there is something very wrong if you're not enjoying yourself.

These years are trickier than they look, however. If they seem daunting, know that you are not alone. It's a deceptively pretty minefield, with minor setbacks and major disasters lurking just beneath the surface. You don't need lessons on how to jump on the mines and blow up your life. If we can make them visible, however, they're easier to avoid. Spray them with fluorescent paint and the challenge of crossing to your thirtieth birthday can become a little easier.

On the far side of their twenties, how do people view the journey? Allow me to don my wizard's cape and conjure a scene from your future. You're sitting at a dining room table with friends and someone asks, "Would you want to be twenty again?"

Laughter ensues, hearty enough to spray wine from the nose.

"Thank God that's over." "Only if I get to keep what I know now." "Body, yes! Brain, no!"

So much work to do. So much to get through. So many mistakes to make.

So what are we doing here? Identifying the wrong turns in the maze. Not all of them, of course. Just forty of the most tempting. May they prove useful.

BACK THROUGH THE TIME TUNNEL

Certain ideas are almost universal. You've probably considered what it might be like to journey back in time to meet an earlier version of yourself. What would you say? What advice would you give? I think of this with every workshop I teach and every book I write: they're meant for younger-me as much as they are for you.

It's all a bit wrongheaded. You can't really prevent all your life mistakes with a book. You couldn't even do so if the time portal opened and a graying version of yourself stepped through, instructions in hand.

My twenty-year-old self would have been defiant to me-the-elder: "You can't tell me what to do. What if you're not really from the future anyway? You might just be trying to control me, make me a good little boy, stuff me back into multiple closets—the obvious one and all the others. You want to extinguish me. No thanks."

Much of it you have to go through on your own. You need direct experience. So, go ahead:

- Trash your best friend behind his back.

- Max out your first credit card.

- Betray your sister's confidence.

- Rebel against people who won't notice you doing it.

- Try to keep a bad relationship going.

- Use your worst temptations as your most trusted guides.

- Wait on the couch for your purpose to be revealed.

- Defend yourself with cool.

Give it a shot. Watch what happens. Learn, not from the pages of this book, but from the cattle prods and taser bursts of real life. No way around it.

Then, if future-you comes back and cautions you against entering a blind alley, perhaps you won't turn away. You may still take a couple of steps into the darkness to see for yourself.

But maybe it'll only be a few steps.

LET'S GET REAL

Misery is not your goal. It isn't mine either. So if you handed me the keys to the time machine, what would I say to my youthful self?

The tempting answer—the one mentioned by more people than anything else—is to say "Don't worry so much." Things will turn out. You'll be fine.

But there's a problem. The only reason to go back is to change the course of history—in this case, to jolt ourselves onto a track other than the one we actually took. But how do we know where that other track would have led? If we had moved to Melbourne we may have been eaten by a great white. If we had married our high school sweetheart they would have divorced us by now. If we had run for that bus we might have slipped beneath its wheels.

The reassurances we give only cover the track we have actually experienced: the life we *have* lived. If I hadn't worried, I would have done different things and experienced different outcomes.

Things in my own life may have worked out only because some of my worry kept me safe. It made me study when another beer was more tempting. It cautioned me against choices even worse than the ones I made. It meant I was prepared when I was asked to give a presentation, defend a thesis, go on a date. It's why I kept friends, saved money, landed jobs, packed bear spray, and never ever (after, all right, one incident in tenth grade) got lost in the woods.

But there is one thing that was no help, and did nothing to keep me safe: despair. The sense that it didn't matter what I did, things were doomed anyway. There was no hope, so no point in trying.

When I was ten years old, an adult regaled me with stories of the upcoming nuclear catastrophe that would wipe us all away. At fifteen, my father's heart attack rocked the family and foretold not only his own death but also my personal genetic heritage. Applying for graduate school, I was convinced I would never be accepted. And then, at twenty-two, came word of a virus that within a few more years began striking friends dead. I remember a supervisor, astonished that one of his contemporaries had collapsed while jogging. I suppressed my envy that he'd reached his forties before his friends started dying.

At each turn I could feel the gravitational pull of despair dragging me to the sofa, to the bed, to the floor. The more I thought about the future, the more diverse the manifestations of doom that appeared.

To be sure, terrible things happened, mostly unanticipated. Having foretold my own death a hundred ways, I'd never considered being struck on my bicycle by a deer launched into the air by a passing car—though that was the one event that almost did the job. But I remain alive, breathing, and happier than in any of my dark visions of the future.

The worry produced despair, and the despair produced nothing. It prevented no tragedy, pushed me toward no goal. Just slowed me down. It had its greatest power in my twenties. Since then it has continued to whisper in my ear occasionally. Like a demented neighbor, it never completely goes away; I just got bored with it and sat down to listen less often.

Neither I nor the world needed my despair. The world doesn't need yours either.

Some will take this to mean that I dismiss the challenges we face as nothing new, nothing too severe, nothing that will actually come to pass. "We're fine. Lighten up!" But most of those past fears became reality. World War I happened, the Great Depression happened, World War II happened, Vietnam happened, the McCarthyism and social constipation of the '50s happened, pollution happened, AIDS happened, 9/11 happened. Climate change, chief among the current concerns facing the world, is happening now, and will certainly intensify.

The challenges of past generations were genuine, not imaginary.

Our world faces the fear of possibility and the dread of certainty. We enter yet another of humanity's long tunnels, not knowing what lies on the other side. There will be deaths, disasters, losses. And there will be, and is now, a demand for people of every living generation to step forward, contribute their voices, make difficult decisions, and work together to meet the challenges of the future. Despair will help none of them.

And your role? The very fact that you are reading this book—that you could afford it, or that a library sits near your home—suggests that you are among the privileged. Not, perhaps, in comparison to the mansion-dwellers across town, but very much so compared to most of the world's population. You have been fed (mostly). You have been kept more or less safe (though probably not infallibly so). Years have been spent educating you, helping you learn to read, add, form sentences, find Italy's boot on the globe.

This makes you a resource. It is not enough to sit on the sidelines, marginalized or feeling so, flipping through screens, consuming products, and feeling dissatisfied. You are needed—perhaps more so than a generation has ever been needed. The world does not have the option of wasting you, and you cannot afford the luxury of wasting yourself. There is much to be done. A world to be helped, an atmosphere to preserve, justice to be served.

Will you save the world? No need to sit in suspense with that question. Of course not. No single soldier ever won a war. Even the famed—Martin Luther King, Marie Curie, Nelson Mandela—would have achieved nothing without the combined efforts of many. No grain of sand makes a beach, no tree constitutes a forest; but without sand and trees there are no beaches, no forests.

"Whatever you do will be insignificant," said Gandhi, "but it is very important that you do it."

In the movie *It's a Wonderful Life*, savings and loan operator George Bailey becomes convinced that his life is overdrawn on the negative side and wishes he had never been born. He discovers, thanks to the intervention of a kindly screenwriter, that his deposits exceed his withdrawals. The world, on balance, is better for his having been there.

One way of looking at the purpose of life is that it is to shrink the debt incurred by our simple existence, then (with luck) to shift the ledger into the black. Positive territory. A plus sign. 0.01, or better.

Simplistic, no? Who's to say what's positive? If you eat an egg, you rob the chicken but feed the farmer. Without your trash the garbage collector would be out of a job. Does your charity donation solve a problem or breed dependence? The case can often be made in any direction. Having a goal of net contribution doesn't solve all problems or alleviate the need for careful consideration. But usually the direction is clear, and having a guidepost helps us make our choices.

This perspective on the question of meaning can sound a bit dull. Shifting our life into beneficial territory means you have to give something. Adulthood sounds like endless work. A positive for the world means a negative for you. As though, having wet ten thousand diapers, you are doomed to wipe the butt of the world until you die.

Well, not quite.

There's a paradox. Reaching your potential, expressing yourself, being your best self, and fulfilling your multiple roles in life, it turns out, are not costs. They're benefits. We pay back the world and wind up with more cash in the emotional wallet than when we started.

It's the passive self, the inert self, that costs us in mood, in energy, in happiness, and in contentment. Ask your focus group of elders to inventory life's best moments. A startling number of their peak experiences will involve trouble taken, not challenges avoided; gifts given, not received. Caring for a child, cooking dinner for friends, using skills in the service of others, joining with colleagues in a common cause. Moments of victory. Shared defeats and setbacks.

This isn't surprising, when you think of it. What is happiness for, after all? It is the brain's chemical reward system. It's designed to be triggered when we act, not when we sit still; when we contribute, not when someone contributes to us. We are social animals, safest among friends, and what is good for the tribe is good for us. We are wired to contribute.

In an increasingly interconnected world, our contribution need not only be to our immediate friends and relatives. It can be to a child half a world away; to an abstraction, like the cure for leukemia; to the inanimate, like the planet itself.

MIRROR IMAGE

So: let's review. Not to worry, it'll only take a moment.

We've been contemplating a photographic negative the whole way. Let's take it into the darkroom and print out its reverse.

- In Part One, we considered the siren song of childhood and whether to remain shut up in the nursery or to pick the lock and escape into adult life. Although the choice seems open, lingering dependency is a denial of reality. If you are a chronological adult, squeezing into childhood clothes will inevitably pinch. To move forward you'll need to relinquish many of the supports to which you have become accustomed, demote your parents from gods to humans, and take on the mantle of adulthood, with all the setbacks and inconvenience that this can entail.

- In Part Two we considered the guiding ideas you have been fed, many of which point into blind alleys. Successful adulthood means carefully sifting through these and discarding the lies in favor of a clear-eyed realism: you're not as special as some may have said, success depends more on effort than talent, pain is a lousy motivator, confidence is the result of action not a prerequisite for it, anger is no privilege, passion is most often cultivated not discovered, and a sense of doom is more often seductive than valid.

- Part Three emphasized that the adult self is largely created, not inherent, and that character is more often the product of conscious rehearsal than of our DNA. Becoming yourself means building a set of skills, overcoming restrictive self-definitions, recognizing your own strength and resilience, experiencing a range of people and settings, exposing your genuine self to the world without disguise, and growing a prefrontal cortex capable of channeling your impulses.

• Once you've created the vessel of a self and lowered it into the water, where do you go? Part Four emphasized the art of navigation: sailing against the tide, making commitments, setting attainable goals, noticing what you have as much as what you lack, maintaining your health, living in the real world, separating needs from wants, recognizing opportunity's knock, and accepting mentorship when needed.

There. Done. Anything else?

CASTING OFF FROM SHORE

Early adulthood is, to a great extent, the process of discovering who you are and displaying this new incarnation to the world. It's easy to sink into self-doubt, convinced that you are uniquely faulty as you discern the many ways you deviate from the norm.

Consider, though. What is personality? What is individuality?

Defining who you are is a matter of tabulating the ways in which you are not average, not standard, not generic. We are tall only in relation to the majority; introverted only in comparison to extroverts; adventurous only by contrast to the herd. Your personality is nothing but the constellation of characteristics that make you abnormal. You can, if you wish, define all of your deviations as dysfunctions, disorders, even diseases. But this makes the erasure of your uniqueness the task of your life. You will turn away from differentness and run to the safety of the average, the indistinct, the normal, the bland.

Instead, at some point, without relinquishing the task of self-creation or the pursuit of life goals, make friends with yourself. Let go of the quest to be what society says you should be, or who your parents or mentors wanted, or even what you once fantasized you would become. Cultivate a sense of peace with who you are. When you reach thirty there is still a long journey ahead, with most of the best that life has to offer. You will be your only constant companion. This should be someone you are happy to be with.

You will never outgrow the need to be your own best friend, your own big sister, your own parent. But eventually it will feel less strange, more automatic. If you become this dual self—the supporter and the supported—you need never be truly alone.

Will you suffer on life's journey? Will you experience misery? Yes.

In the field of artificial intelligence, one of the most vexing problems is how one might discern the presence of consciousness in a human-made system. Is there a question that, if answered accurately, would confirm that consciousness exists?

Buddhists argue that this is an easy one. "Do you suffer?" A conscious being is one that experiences suffering. It comes with the territory. No suffering? Not conscious.

But there is another layer to the problem. A peculiar design flaw in humans is the rejection of suffering: the attempt to eliminate it, suppress it, distance oneself from it. This acts like a magnifying glass on the suffering already present.

To reduce your suffering, stop struggling against this essential ingredient in the soup of life. Accept it. You will not eliminate suffering this way—but you will stop making it worse.

AND ONE MORE THING

A single image from this book remains. It recurs again and again as I see people in early adulthood. The waiting room. The one with a thousand doors, all of them closed, looking firmly locked, requiring someone bigger, smarter, stronger, to come along and produce a key ring.

I sit in the rafters above, looking down at my client sitting there, feeling stuck. I hold no keys. All I have is the knowledge that most of those doors, however they might appear, are actually unlocked.

I don't need to jimmy any latches. I just have to encourage my client to stand, walk to any door, and try the knob. And if it's one of the few that leads nowhere, to try another. Everything will flow from that.

I sat in that waiting room myself in my early twenties, at times feeling blocked on every front. I see now that the bolts and barricades were mostly in my own mind. I wondered, back then, when I would feel like an adult, like a grown man, like a finished product—not a boy, an imposter, a half-wired human.

Adult? Man? Those two sank in eventually.

But finished? Doesn't happen.

You will never really become who you are. You will only continue the process of becoming.

Good luck.

Acknowledgments

This book is a compilation of ideas, insights, metaphors, and experiences gathered from multiple sources—in the literature, on the water, in the consulting room, on the trail, in coffee shops and pubs, and on the long trek through a career rich in friendship and discussion. I am privileged to be surrounded by a diverse and contradictory group of influencers, and can lay genuine claim only to any errors that have found their way onto these pages.

As always, it is to my clients, past and present, to whom I owe many of the thoughts that have found their way into this book. Their efforts, struggles, and openness are an ongoing inspiration.

Immersion in a writing project inevitably seeps into everyday conversation, and I am thankful for the tolerance shown by so many. Special thanks to Luke H., Sanders W., Lorne B., and Greg B. are in order, as well as to Ben C., launched into yet another new world.

The Changeways Clinic team has provided more collegiality, friendship, and insight than one could hope for. Many thanks to Ekin Blackwell, Martha Capréol, Mair Cayley, Sarah Cockell, Alana Cook, Nicole Dorfan, Anne Howson, Mahesh Menon, Sylvia Nay, Nancy Prober, Hajera Rostam, Suja Srikameswaran, Lindsey Thomas, Adrienne Wang, Quincy Young, and, of course, Heather Capocci, who keeps us all in line. I'd also like to thank my earlier mentors, including the late Anne Treisman, as well as Richard W. J. Neufeld, Bill Newby, and Dan Bilsker.

The team at New Harbinger Publications has, as always, been stellar. Thank you to Tesilya Hanauer for shepherding the project through, as well as to Caleb Beckwith, Teja Watson, and Amy Shoup. Thanks go as well to all those who contributed to the success of my earlier book, *How to Be Miserable: 40 Strategies You Already Use,* including the many reviewers, media, podcast hosts, and YouTubers (particularly C.G.P. Grey) who took it to heart.

The primary burden, as usual, has fallen to Geoff B., adviser, Buddhist consultant, and husband, who has been extremely tolerant of absenteeism and unmown fields. A lifetime is not enough.

References and Additional Reading

Adams, R. 1972. *Watership Down*. London: Rex Collings.

American Psychiatric Association. 2013. *Diagnostic and Statistical Manual of Mental Disorders*. 5th ed. Arlington, VA: American Psychiatric Publishing, Inc.

Arnett, J. J., and E. Fishel. 2013. *Getting to 30: A Parent's Guide to the 20-Something Years*. New York: Workman Publishing.

Bandelow, B., and S. Michaelis. 2015. "Epidemiology of Anxiety Disorders in the 21st Century." *Dialogues in Clinical Neuroscience* 17: 327–335.

Bly, R. 1990. *Iron John: A Book about Men*. Reading, MA: Addison-Wesley.

Brown, K. W. 2018. *Adulting: How to Become a Grown-up in 535 Easy-ish Steps*. Updated ed. New York: Hachette.

Campbell, J. 2008. *The Hero with a Thousand Faces*. 3rd ed. New York: New World.

Campbell, J., and B. Moyers. 1991. *The Power of Myth*. New York: Anchor.

Crisp, Q. 1975. *How to Have a Lifestyle*. London: Cecil Woolf Publishers.

Ehrenreich, B. 2009. *Bright-Sided: How Positive Thinking Is Undermining America*. New York: Metropolitan Books.

Erikson, E. H. 1994. *Identity and the Life Cycle*. New York: W. W. Norton.

Freud, S. 1978. *The Standard Edition of the Complete Psychological Works of Sigmund Freud*. Vol. XIX. London: Hogarth Press.

Gilbert, D. 2006. *Stumbling on Happiness*. New York: Random House.

Hall, G. S. 1904. *Adolescence: Its Psychology and Its Relations to Physiology, Anthropology, Sociology, Sex, Crime, Religion. and Education*. Vols. I and II. New York: D. Appleton & Co.

Jay, M. 2012. *The Defining Decade*. New York: Twelve.

Koslow, S. 2013. *Slouching toward Adulthood*. New York: Penguin.

Mahler, M. S., F. Pine, and A. Bergman. 2008. *The Psychological Birth of the Human Infant: Symbiosis and Individuation*. New York: Basic Books.

Mischel, W. 2015. *The Marshmallow Test: Why Self-Control Is the Engine of Success*. New York: Back Bay Books.

Nielsen Company. 2018. "The Nielsen Total Audience Report."

Paterson, R. 2000. *The Assertiveness Workbook: How to Express Your Ideas and Stand Up for Yourself at Work and in Relationships*. Oakland, CA: New Harbinger Publications.

Paterson, R. J. 2016. *How to Be Miserable: 40 Strategies You Already Use*. Oakland, CA: New Harbinger Publications.

Peeters, A., J. J. Barendregt, F. Willekens, J. P. Mackenbach, A. Al Mamun, L. Bonneux, et al. 2003. "Obesity in Adulthood and Its Consequences for Life Expectancy: A Life-Table Analysis." *Annals of Internal Medicine* 138(1): 24–32.

Rogers, C. 1951. *Client-Centered Therapy: Its Current Practice, Implications, and Theory.* London: Constable.

Sax, L. 2007. *Boys Adrift.* New York: Basic Books.

Tajan, N., H. Yukiko, and N. Pionnié-Dax. 2017. "Hikikomori: The Japanese Cabinet Office's 2016 Survey of Acute Social Withdrawal." *Asia Pacific Journal* 15: 115.

Treisman, A., and R. Paterson. 1984. "Emergent Features, Attention, and Object Perception." *Journal of Experimental Psychology: Human Perception and Performance* 10: 12–31.

US Department of Health and Human Services. 2014. "The Health Consequences of Smoking—50 Years of Progress: A Report of the Surgeon General." Washington DC: US Department of Health and Human Services, Centers for Disease Control and Prevention, National Center for Chronic Disease Prevention and Health Promotion, Office on Smoking and Health.

Endnotes

1   Erik Erikson, *Identity and the Life Cycle* (New York: W. W. Norton, 1994).

2   C. G. P. Grey, "7 Ways to Maximize Misery," www.youtube.com/watch?v=LO1mTELoj6o&t=370s.

3   G. Stanley Hall, *Adolescence: Its Psychology and Its Relations to Physiology, Anthropology, Sociology, Sex, Crime, Religion, and Education* (New York: D. Appleton & Co., 1904).

4   Borwin Bandelow and Sophie Michaelis, "Epidemiology of Anxiety Disorders in the 21st Century," *Dialogues in Clinical Neuroscience* 17 (2015): 327–335.

5   American Psychiatric Association, *Diagnostic and Statistical Manual of Mental Disorders*, 5th ed. (Arlington, VA: American Psychiatric Publishing, Inc., 2013).

6   Cited in Nicolas Tajan, Hamasaki Yukiko, and Nancy Pionnié-Dax, "Hikikomori: The Japanese Cabinet Office's 2016 Survey of Acute Social Withdrawal," *Asia Pacific Journal: Japan Focus* 15 (2017): 1–15.

7   Figures are for 2017. Eurostat Statistics on Income and Living Conditions, ec.europa.eu/eurostat/cache/metadata/en/ilc_esms.htm.

8   Richard Fry, "It's Becoming More Common for Young Adults to Live at Home—and For Longer Stretches", (Washington, DC: Pew Research Center, 2017). www.pewresearch.org/fact-tank

/2017/05/05/its-becoming-more-common-for-young-adults
-to-live-at-home-and-for-longer-stretches.

9   US Bureau of Labor Statistics, "American Time Use Survey" (2017).

10 Nielsen Company, "The Nielsen Total Audience Report Q2" (2018).

11 US Department of Health and Human Services, "The Health Consequences of Smoking—50 Years of Progress: A Report of the Surgeon General, Atlanta" (Washington, DC: US Department of Health and Human Services, Centers for Disease Control and Prevention, National Center for Chronic Disease Prevention and Health Promotion, Office on Smoking and Health, 2014).

12 Anna Peeters, Jan J. Barendregt, Frans Willekens, Johan Mackenbach, Abdullah Al Mamun, Luke Bonneux, et al., "Obesity in Adulthood and Its Consequences for Life Expectancy: A Life-Table Analysis," *Annals of Internal Medicine* 138(1) (2003): 24–32.

13 Carl Rogers, *Client-Centered Therapy: Its Current Practice, Implications, and Theory* (London: Constable, 1951).

14 Sigmund Freud, *The Standard Edition of the Complete Psychological Works of Sigmund Freud*, Vol. XIX (London: Hogarth Press, 1978).

15 Walter Mischel, *The Marshmallow Test: Why Self-Control Is the Engine of Success* (New York: Back Bay Books, 2015).

16 Anne Treisman and Randolph Paterson, "Emergent Features, Attention, and Object Perception," *Journal of Experimental Psychology: Human Perception and Performance* 10 (1984): 12–31.

Randy J. Paterson, PhD, is a psychologist and director of Changeways Clinic—a private psychotherapy service—in Vancouver, BC, Canada. He is author of *The Assertiveness Workbook*, *How to Be Miserable*, and *Your Depression Map*; and coauthor of the free online *Antidepressant Skills Workbook*. He presents lectures and workshops internationally on topics, including mental health policy, cognitive behavioral therapy (CBT), the nature and treatment of depression and anxiety disorders, and the failure-to-launch phenomenon. For more information, visit www.randypaterson.com.

MORE BOOKS *from*
NEW HARBINGER PUBLICATIONS

HOW TO BE MISERABLE

40 Strategies You Already Use

978-1626254060

US $15.95

THE MINDFUL TWENTY-SOMETHING

Life Skills to Handle Stress... & Everything Else

978-1626254893

US $16.95

EMBRACE YOUR GREATNESS

Fifty Ways to Build Unshakable Self-Esteem

978-1684032204

US $16.95

ANXIETY HAPPENS

52 Ways to Find Peace of Mind

978-1684031108

US $14.95

MASTERING ADULTHOOD

Go Beyond Adulting to Become an Emotional Grown-Up

978-1684031931

US $16.95

HEALTHY HABITS SUCK

How to Get Off the Couch & Live a Healthy Life... Even If You Don't Want To

978-1684033317

US $16.95

 newharbingerpublications
1-800-748-6273 / newharbinger.com

(VISA, MC, AMEX / prices subject to change without notice)   Follow Us

Sign up for book alerts! **Go to newharbinger.com/bookalerts**